ON
TARGET

ON TARGET

HOW THE WORLD'S HOTTEST RETAILER HIT A BULL'S-EYE

Laura Rowley

WILEY

John Wiley & Sons, Inc.

Published by John Wiley & Sons, Inc., Hoboken, New Jersey
Published simultaneously in Canada.

For general information on our other products and services, or technical support,
please contact our Customer Care Department within the United States at
800-762-2974, outside the United States at 317-572-3993 or fax 317-572-4002.

Wiley also publishes its books in a variety of electronic formats. Some content that
appears in print may not be available in electronic books.

For more information about Wiley products, visit our web site at www.wiley.com.

Library of Congress Cataloging-in-Publication Data:

Rowley, Laura.
 On Target : how the world's hottest retailer hit a bull's-eye / Laura Rowley.
     p. cm.
 Published simultaneously in Canada.
 Includes index.
  ISBN 0-471-25067-8 (cloth : alk. paper)
 1. Target Corporation. 2. Dayton, George Draper, 1857–1938. I. Title.
 HF5465.U64 T377 2003
 381'.141'0973—dc21

                                                    2002153128

Printed in the United States of America

10 9 8 7 6 5 4 3 2 1

Contents

Acknowledgments

Thanks to Debra Wishik Englander, my editor at John Wiley & Sons, who called me with the idea for *On Target*. I am grateful for your confidence, support, and patience throughout the writing of this book. I could not have told the story without the generous cooperation of Bruce and Douglas Dayton, who sat for long interviews and provided crucial resources on the history of Target Corporation and the Dayton family. Thanks to Dayton Hudson executives Norman McMillan, Allan Pennington, Stephen Pistner and Floyd Hall for sharing their stories with me; and Marc Gobé for his invaluable insight. I am indebted to librarians Sandra Date at the *Minneapolis Star Tribune*, Susan Pistilli and Mike Tubridy at the International Council of Shopping Centers and Heather Martin at Lebhar Friedman for their research assistance. Thank you to my parents, Jane and Eugene Rowley, and my extended family for your faith in me. To my husband Jim Hilker, and daughters Anne, Charlotte, and Holly: Thank you for your love. When I count my blessings, I always count you twice.

Introduction

In early 2000, as a producer for CNN business news, I interviewed Edward Yardeni, chief economist with Deutsche Bank. The stock market was booming, unemployment had hit an historic low and Osama bin Laden wasn't even on the radar screen. Yardeni, hailed as an economic visionary, argued that competition and globalization had led to zero inflation, strong growth, and peace. Then he said something that struck me as so preposterously simple I'll never forget it: "Other countries have discovered that the meaning of life is shopping." Shopping? That's what it all boils down to?

When the world fell apart on September 11, 2001, shopping remained, in many ways, central to the meaning of life, at least in the United States. President Bush, New York Mayor Giuliani, and other leaders urged Americans to support the economy and fight terrorism by spending money (an equation some people found disturbing). But spend they did—the powerful consumer propped up the economy despite a tanking stock market, swiftly rising unemployment, and a drastic decline in corporate spending. Consumers spent their cash at two places, primarily: home improvement chains and discounters. (When they did buy at upscale stores, it was small luxuries. Federated Department Stores, which include Macy's and Bloomingdale's, registered a huge jump in sales of lipstick in the weeks after 9/11.) When the going gets tough, apparently, the tough really do go shopping.

But why do they shop at Target? Almost everyone I interviewed for this book told me they have an inchoate longing to go there. They feel good roaming the aisles of the discounter but can't explain why. On the surface, of course, they mention the whimsical merchandise, cool ads, clean stores, fast service, and community giving. But as a former seminary student, I was as intrigued by the internal experience as the external one. What are the psychological implications for the consumer in the way Target does business? Branding expert Marc Gobé describes it as the human touch: "We are living in a time where we are losing control of our own lives—technologies move faster than we do—and globalization is a concept that is very hard to completely embrace," he said. "People are seeking somehow to be reassured with anything that has some kind of human touch. Target delivers the human touch through communication, through their products, through the design of their stores and their people. You feel that personal touch and feel reassured in a world that's not reassuring."

American are hungry not only for reassurance, but for values, according to consultants Fred Crawford and Ryan Mathews, authors of *The Myth of Excellence: Why Great Companies Never Try to Be the Best at Everything* (Crown Business, 2001). "For the first time in history, businesses are being asked to do something other than engage in commerce," they state. "Customers increasingly frustrated with the experience of their lives want reinforcement of personal—not just commercial—values." The two argue that traditional social institutions—religion, schools, neighborhoods, family life—that once reinforced universal values of honesty, dignity, and fair play are breaking down. Certainly after their book was published, capitalism itself seemed to be collapsing under the weight of runaway greed. Americans were treated to the successive spectacles of accounting scandals and outright fraud at Enron, Arthur Andersen, Worldcom, Tyco, and Adelphia Communications, to name just a few—betrayals that devastated shareholders, workers, and the community alike.

In my research for this book, I had the privilege of interviewing Douglas and Bruce Dayton, two of the five brothers who ran Dayton's and launched Target stores in the 1960s. The brothers are of the same generation as John Rigas, the Adelphia Communications founder, who federal prosecutors accused, with his sons, of using the company as a "personal piggy bank." When I asked Douglas Dayton why he and his brothers never had a similar temptation, he replied, "It wasn't the way we were brought up. How could you do that to the people there?" Rather than holding fast to their power, the Dayton brothers focused on making the board the dominant factor in the company. "We had the board reviewing the CEO, and his bonus depended on it," Bruce Dayton said. "Not many companies do that. Most of the CEOs who have gone out of line have been big egos that haven't been reviewed, and haven't felt they were accountable to anybody." (When profits declined in the early 1970s, then-CEO Kenneth Dayton even went to the board and offered to resign.) I came to believe that a key part of Target's success today is the culture of integrity that nurtured it through its first two decades of growth. "Father said it was all right to have all of your eggs in one basket when you take good care of that basket," said Bruce Dayton. "And he imbued us with the idea that you couldn't milk the company. Take good care of it, it will take care of you. That was our heritage." In the process, they took care of many others. In 2002, Target's 40th anniversary, Doug Dayton ran into a company old-timer in the checkout lane of a suburban Minneapolis Target store. The sharp-eyed cashier caught the name on his credit card, looked around, leaned toward him and confided, "I bought three shares, and they're worth ten thousand dollars!"

Crawford and Mathews argue that the search for values, like nature, abhors a vacuum—and people are looking to commerce to fill the void. Why do people gravitate to Target? When quality products are offered at a fair price, it implies honesty; someone respects the value of your hard-earned dollar. When a store is clean, well-organized, and gets you on your way quickly, it implies respect for your time. When the products are imaginative and stylish, it implies a belief that everyone, not just the wealthy, appreciates and deserves beauty. Giving away $100 million a year implies that someone shares your concerns about the community. The external experience is about shopping; the internal, emotional experience is about being validated, and treated with respect. This book will look at how the company's history planted the seeds for Target's culture; how it reinvented the discount store concept, carving a niche that would allow it to thrive even in the shadow of industry giant Wal-Mart; and how its best practices in management, merchandising, marketing, operations, and corporate giving have combined to make it one of the most successful retailers of the new millennium—in short, how Target hit the bull's-eye.

CHAPTER 1

The Target Difference

When I go into a competitor's store,
I have this uncontrollable urge to get what
I need and get the heck out. With Target,
it's more like, "Stick around for a
while, relax."

—Curtis Chan, Target customer

THE NEW DISCOUNT SHOPPER

The grand ballroom of the Waldorf Astoria in midtown Manhattan is overflowing with proper Chanel suits, pearls, coiffed hair and the tight smiles characteristic of expensive plastic surgery. Several hundred women gather to hear Libby Pataki, the then-first lady of New York, discuss the state's efforts to fight ovarian and breast cancer. The event, which includes a fashion show, will raise $650,000 for a center that provides mammograms to low-income women. The tables are teeming with white linen, pearly china adorned with cold pink salmon and asparagus in light vinaigrette, crystal stemware filled with mellow chardonnay. The crowd is sprinkled with younger, hipper attendees as well, including Charla Krupp, a longtime magazine editor and regular contributor to "The Today Show." She is seated across from Pia Lieb, a Madison Avenue celebrity dentist who has catered to her clientele's unique desires in pioneering ways, including bonding "healing crystals" into their teeth. When I mention the Target Corporation, the two women launch into heated declarations of their devotion with the enthusiasm of apostles encountering the risen messiah. "I went to the Target in Setauket (New York)," Krupp said. "I came out with two shopping carts full of stuff. They had to help me out the door. It's so cheap! It's amazing!" Realizing she hadn't gotten everything she needed as she drove back to Manhattan, Krupp said she called Target on her cell phone to get directions to the store nearest to the Long Island Expressway—in Westbury, where she filled another cart. Lieb tells Krupp she should check out the two-story Target in Queens, because it is geographically the closest to Manhattan (she measured on a map). "I take the subway out there," Lieb gushed. "Then if I buy too much stuff, I call a car service to pick me up at the store." The two are rapturous as they extol the virtues of Target's trendy housewares.

THE NEW DISCOUNT DESIGNER

Inside a nondescript brick building on the west side of Manhattan, more than a dozen crewmembers are scurrying around a cavernous dark space. This moving mass of headphones, wires, and cameras prepares to shoot an episode of "Everyday Elegance with Colin Cowie," the signature style show on the Women's Entertainment Network. Host Cowie, a lifestyle guru who has planned parties for Tom Cruise and Jerry Seinfeld, looks for all the world like he's just stepped out of a James Bond movie—a buff, youthful Sean Connery, in black turtleneck and slim-cut trousers, dazzling white smile. Cowie, a native of Zambia schooled in South Africa, designed the show's spare, contemporary set. It is stripped of the usual talk show clichés—the overstuffed couch, flowers, bookcases with pewter candlesticks. Instead, warm colors are projected on muted gray walls, an austere staircase adorned only with three dress forms curves up to a platform, and guests lounge in 1960s swivel club chairs, upholstered in a soft black velvet on a stark aluminum base.

Cowie has edged away from his bread-and-butter business— event planning—and into media and product design, including an exclusive line of china for Lenox. Cowie mentions that he spoke with Target about designing a collection of housewares, but backed away when the retailer proposed a one-year deal. "When you're at this stage in your career, you want more of a commitment," he said in his clipped South African accent.

Perhaps a dozen years ago, the idea of a well-heeled New Yorker shopping at a discount store would have been ludicrous; even more so, a celebrity designer seeking a long-term commitment. "Mass" retail was a four-letter word. One only had to recall the fate of those who dared to cross the status barrier: the licensing catastrophe that turned couture designer Pierre Cardin into a marketer of cheap socks and cologne; Halston's 1982 collection for J.C. Penney that decimated his high-end business. But the 1990s saw a seismic shift in the retail landscape, one so powerful that by the turn of the century, a Midwestern discount store would capture even the imagination of Manhattan's fashionistas—the world's rarified uber-consumers, insatiable and capricious, embracing and abandoning new style like carrion crows. Target's executives are shrewd strategists who have spent decades pursuing the upper-middle class; so when Americans began to focus on value, and fashion became more democratic, Target was prepared to capitalize on the sea change.

CAPTURING THE UPSCALE BARGAIN HUNTER

To shoppers in major cities in the Northeast, Target is a startling new phenomenon that appeared out of nowhere in the mid-1990s. But the store's virtues have been appreciated for years in the Midwest, where the chain was born. Target is just over four decades old—but its roots sink deep into the soil of the 1900s, the era of the great merchants in a pioneering and optimistic America—including an energetic entrepreneur named George Draper Dayton. He founded Dayton's department store in Minneapolis and built a reputation for quality goods, low prices, excellent service—including a liberal return policy—and scrupulous honesty (a customer who could find an inaccurate advertisement was awarded a dollar). Dayton's grandsons founded Target in 1962, consciously crafting a culture infused with the parent company's values—but wisely freeing the chain to innovate in its own way. In 1969, Dayton's merged with J.L. Hudson Company, a Detroit-based department store, and became Dayton Hudson—but its future lay in discounting. By 2000, Dayton Hudson operated three main divisions: discount stores, upscale department stores, and a mid-range department store called Mervyn's. That year, Target stores contributed a whopping 83 percent of the company's pretax profits, and on January 30, 2000, Dayton Hudson finally acknowledged its crown jewel: It changed its name to Target Corporation. Over four decades, through its edgy products, innovative store design, memorable image campaigns, and remarkably generous philanthropy, the discount chain with the trademark bull's-eye has developed a cult-like following among American shoppers. "Tar-zhay"—in the faux French pronunciation preferred by

Target Corporation: Divisions

Name of division	Description	Percentage of pretax profit
Target	Discount store in three formats: a standard store; Target Greatland, a larger version with a pharmacy, one-hour photo and other features; SuperTarget, a larger store containing a 50,000-sq.-ft. supermarket	85.86
Marshall Field's	Upscale Department Stores, including former Dayton's and Hudson's stores	4.49
Mervyn's	Mid-range department store, primarily in the Midwest and West	9.65
Target.direct	Websites and catalogs	0

Source: 2001 Annual Report

middle- and-upper-income clients—sells bargains *and* cachet. Target made it hip to be spare.

THE TARGET EXPERIENCE

To understand why Target is so different from its rivals, consider the dark lesson taught by the worst mass retailers in the United States: You can save money in a discount store as long as you can endure the misery—pushy crowds, overhead noise, dirt and clutter, offensive lighting, racks jammed with a single size, labyrinth-like layouts, insolent salespeople, and excruciating checkout lines. Come inside, save a few dimes, just don't forget who you are: the Rodney Dangerfield of consumers. You get no respect here. Discount shopping can make you feel genuinely inferior. In your heart you know the truth: Real consumers shop at Bloomingdale's.

Then you stumble into a Target. The experience is remarkable mainly for what is missing. First, the noise: There is no Muzak, no loudspeaker static. It is the mystical feeling of being alone in your own head, without the greatest hits of the '80s evoking bad prom memories. The lighting is bright, inviting—no garish industrial fluorescents. Grab a cherry red shopping cart and begin tooling around the store. There is no obstacle course: No dump bins on wheels to block the way; no merchandise spilled on the floor; no intimidating pallets of product towering twenty feet high, threatening serious head injuries. You've got your basic optical, pharmacy, and photofinishing departments, and if you're in a SuperTarget, there is a Starbucks boutique and an E*TRADE financial zone, where you can sip a latte while you do banking or trade stocks. When another customer heads your way, there is no shopping-cart jousting match because the aisles are wide enough to accommodate at least two carts. To your surprise, you are not disoriented. Overhead signs in a gigantic typeface and strong primary colors designate the various departments. In every section there is a bright red phone, your very own Batphone. Can't find the eyeliner? There's a live superhero on the line to guide you safely to cosmetics.

"Before I was a professor, I worked at a housewares distribution company which sold to Target," said Michael Levy, a professor of retailing at Babson College in Massachusetts and co-editor of the *Journal of Retailing*. "They were always very clean, very well-lit, very spacious. You know the saying, 'retail is detail'? They always paid a lot of attention to detail. Their stores always looked a lot better than the discount store competition. Even though the shelves were stacked a little higher and the displays were not as slick as department stores, they looked more like department stores in those days than the sort of dark, dingy look of a discount store."

Dina Brachman, a marketing executive for a global pharmaceutical firm, spends $400 a month on everything from cat food to laundry detergent at a Target in New Jersey. "Target has intimacy, great merchandising, I can actually find what I need and it's priced," she said. "It's like a mix between a true discounter and a regular department store. We never had Wal-Mart, so when they [Wal-Mart] came here, I thought, oh good, maybe they have better prices. It was dreadful. I've been there twice and hated every minute of it. It's dirty, it's big, it's disorganized, it's a warehouse. And it's horribly merchandised."

Curtis Chan, who works in public relations for Pennsylvania State University in University Park, remembers buying his first G.I. Joe action figure at a Target in the 1970s. He rediscovered it in the 1990s. "My first impression of the store is that it's very clean and welcoming. When I go into a competitor's store, I don't feel nearly as comfortable and have this uncontrollable urge to get what I need and get the heck out. No browsing. With Target, it's more like, 'Stick around for a while, relax.' "

A FLAIR FOR DESIGN

But customers obviously don't come just for the environment. They come for the merchandise. This—the stuff on the shelves—is where Target differs most significantly from competitors. It's fun, distinctive, smart, sophisticated, even entertaining. There are a few names you may have heard before—Michael Graves, Mossimo, Calphalon, Todd Oldham, Stride Rite—but even if the names are unfamiliar, you know good design when you see it. And it's grouped, thoughtfully: In housewares, one row displays a collection of lamp bases, and just above, an assortment of lamp shades—hey, someone has confidence in your ability to mix and match. It might be a department store, except everything is so cheap. At checkout, a platoon of cashiers awaits, making your exit swift.

"I'm beyond obsessed with Target," said Tory Johnson, a well-to-do Manhattan business owner who takes her five-year-old twins to a store every weekend, alternating between suburban New York and New Jersey. "My favorite section is the front of the store where they have the seasonal stuff. I probably spent close to $5,000 between the two stores—that's not so insignificant in just over three months. My favorite Christmas item was the faux mercury-style candlesticks. I wiped out the Edgewater (New Jersey) store and then drove all the way to Long Island and bought all of their stock, too. They were the best presents for under $10. I sent them with pillar candles to 60 people who would never have gotten a gift from me if I didn't flip over how great and inexpensive these were." Right after the holidays, Valentine's goodies replaced the Christmas stock. "I went wild!" said Johnson, who estimates she brings home more bags from Target each week than from grocery stores. "I bought just about all of the decorations for my kids' class and our home. In fact, I had a Valentine's Social for 15 five-year-olds just so I had an excuse to buy all this fabulous pink and red stuff. Now I'm into all the St. Patrick's and Easter things—never mind that I'm Jewish."

Brachman, a mother of two, is also a big fan of Target's playful seasonal wares. "Everything we got for Halloween was Target— pumpkins, purple skeletons—it's great stuff," she said. "I bought a great set of picnic dishes because they were so much fun, so bright and zippy-looking. I have lots of picnics in my backyard. I made myself very happy for $35."

Target's seasonal housewares are emblematic of the corporation's strategy: It has invested in technology and warehouse facilities to manage the supply chain and shorten inventory lead times, so the shelves look fresh and remain in-stock. At the same time, merchandise turns over frequently, creating in shoppers an urgency to buy now, and come back often to see what's new. "When you see something cute you better grab it—because you won't see it again," said Dallas Target shopper Melodie Layman. "I'm more prone to go ahead and purchase even if I think I may not need it, because I'll go back and it's gone. I almost always keep it."

Moreover, Target is also one of the first retailers to use real-time Customer Relationship Management systems to improve service. If Tory Johnson or Melodie Layman make purchases in the store, on the Internet and from a catalog, and then call customer service, the representative on the phone will have an immediate record of all their transactions. Moreover, Target's website is strongly focused on deepening the customer relationship and building the brand, rather than simply driving sales. (See Chapter 5.)

To get upscale shoppers to notice in the store in the first place, Target had to make a splash with its advertising. The chain announced its arrival in the competitive Northeast with a series of award-winning ads that focused on the red bull's-eye logo, and mixed substance with style. (See Chapter 4.) In addition, the chain spends millions on promotions that associate it with the nation's style makers. Bob Dzienis, a 30-year-old advertising executive, said Target's ads lured him into a New Jersey store, where he became a true believer. "Target's image campaign is unbelievable. I love their ads. You see these ads, and go into the store, and think, 'Hey there's cool stuff in here.' And you just want to stay there. I could stay there for two hours." Dzienis also praises the customer service. "These [Target] people seem knowledgeable about the products, or if not they'll go find somebody who is," he noted. "They have a more positive attitude in interactions I've seen with customers." Target monitors staff responsiveness to its "guests" electronically and through surveys. In the early 1990s, Target adopted some of Walt Disney's staff training and customer service initiatives. It has since developed a variety of methods—from hiring to coaching to grading performance—to ensure "team members" embody the motto "fast, fun and friendly." (See Chapter 5.)

Marc Gobé, founder of the New York City branding and design firm Desgrippes Gobé Group, contends that Target delivers a human touch in an impersonal and uncertain world. Gobé, coauthor of *Emotional Branding: The New Paradigm for Connecting Brands to People* (Allworth Press, 2001) explained in the thick accent of his native Paris, "We have evolved from an industrial-based economy to a people economy, where factories are not heroes anymore, but people are the heroes. When Henry Ford said, 'You can have any color [model-T automobile] as long as it's black,' it showed the arrogance of this era. In the modern emotional economy, what's interesting is that people are looking to brands for solutions for their lives. We are living in a time where we are losing control of our own lives—technologies move faster than we do—and globalization is a concept that is very hard to completely embrace. The isolation in which everybody lives is somewhat frightening. The change in demographics—in which the construct of the traditional family represents only 28 percent of the population—has been destabilizing to people. People are seeking some-how to be reassured with anything that has some kind of human touch. Brands that deliver this human aspect of communication are being preferred."

Target delivers on the emotional experience for several reasons: it has a vision for its products that focuses on superior design; the company's internal culture is geared toward the customer; and it communicates its image in a visual language that reflects its values. In other words, the holy trinity of a winning business model: product, service, image—along with a fourth element that is becoming increasingly important to customers, philanthropy. Since 1946, the corporation has given 5 percent of its pretax profits to charity. In 2002, Target handed out roughly $2 million a week to communities where it does business, supporting the arts, education, environment, and other causes. Target marries marketing and philanthropy in clever ways—the School Fundraising program, for example, allows Target credit card holders to designate a school to receive 1 percent of their purchases every time they use the card. "I got my charge card just for that," said customer Dina Brachman. (See Chapter 10.)

Those attributes, which we will explore in this book, have made Target the home of the upscale bargain hunter. Consider the chain's demographics: At 44, Target's average client is younger than most discount shoppers and college educated, with a household income approaching $50,000. She—four of five customers are female—also drops a bigger hunk of wallet at the store than at rivals. When her income crosses $100,000, she shops almost exclusively at Target for her discount purchases. As Salomon Smith Barney analyst Deborah Weinswig notes: "You will see a person in a pair of Ferragamos in Target—you will not see that in Wal-Mart."

That's not to say Wal-Mart hasn't recognized Target's success and made a solid effort to lure Ferragamo-shod clients into its big boxes. Wal-Mart, in fact, has been a devout student of Target's gospel of affordable flair, and now claims to be a convert, hiring dozens of designers from stores like The Limited to upgrade its apparel offerings, and stocking Godiva white chocolate raspberry ice cream in the freezer next to Sam's Choice in markets such as Alpharetta, Georgia and Plano, Texas. But over four decades, Target has made stylishness a core competency, honing its merchandising expertise, external resources, store design, and service standards—not to mention flashy image campaigns—to support that competency; just as surely as Wal-Mart has developed the logistics and distribution skills to become the most cost-efficient retailer on the planet. Wal-Mart, which is the nation's largest seller of apparel, may have Target in its crosshairs, but for the down-home discounter to actually compete on Target's turf would take a cultural and image revolution—one that would risk alienating its traditional customers, who are far more interested in saving hard-earned money on toilet paper and snack food than seeking a Mossimo tee to pair with Armani slacks, or a Michael Graves toaster to complement a stainless steel Sub-Zero refrigerator. In the next chapter, we'll learn about the products and unique merchandising strategies that have made Target one of the most successful retailers in the United States.

⊙ CHECK OUT

The Target Difference

"Expect more. Pay less": Whimsical, well-designed, affordable products—especially in housewares and apparel—turn over quickly, so customers return frequently.

"Fast, fun and friendly": Smartly uniformed "team members" are trained, monitored, and given feedback on the quality of their service to "guests."

Welcoming environment: Stores have an easy-to-navigate racetrack floorplan, wide, clean aisles, pleasing lighting, no Muzak, unambiguous signage, maps, customer service phones, well-organized displays of complementary merchandise, and numerous check-out lanes.

Image campaign: Distinctive advertising combines a sophisticated visual sensibility and humorous execution; sponsorships connect the chain with trendsetters in fashion, sports, and so on.

Philanthropy: Target has a long-standing policy of giving away 5 percent of pretax income—roughly $100 million in 2002. Its "cause marketing" is clever and highly successful; for example, it links school donations to its credit card business.

Technology: Sophisticated technology controls the flow of information and inventory so stores stay in-stock on the hottest items; Customer Relationship Management systems give real-time data from all of the company's sales channels, helping improve service.

Heritage: Target was founded by Dayton's, a department store chain, giving the discounter an upscale sensibility and a legacy of strong values.

CHAPTER 2

The Right Stuff

They are really at the top of the list
when people are talking about where
to register for bridal gifts right now—so
it's the right kind of product with the right
kind of retail environment.

—Rick Goings, chairman
and CEO, Tupperware

THE NAME BRAND GAME

When Target was formed in the early 1960s, the chain's founders publicly claimed the upper end of the discount business for themselves. "We will offer high-quality merchandise at low margins because we are cutting expenses," Douglas Dayton declared at the opening of the first Target in Roseville, Minnesota, in the spring of 1962. "We would much rather do this than trumpet dramatic price cuts on cheap merchandise."[1] Today, Target employs a multiprong retailing strategy to stay ahead of the style game: It works with major brands to develop exclusive, affordable collections for Target; it manufactures its own private label goods, gathering ideas from internal and external consultants; and it arranges licensing deals with innovative designers who are not necessarily celebrities, but whose artistic vision spearheads Target's quest to differentiate itself from other discounters.

In the early years, Target couldn't get the hot brand names. Mass was crass: Companies kept their goods out of discounters to protect their elite images, and those who dared to traverse the line suffered. In 1982, the fashion designer Halston—the icon known for the pillbox hat worn by Jackie Kennedy in the 1960s and the slinky look of Studio 54 in the 1970s—created an affordable collection for J.C. Penney. The move devastated Halston's couture business, as Bergdorf Goodman and other stores promptly dropped his line. Today, on the other hand, name brand apparel can often be found in a warehouse store, an outlet, or a discounter. But back in 1979, this was rare, and when Target acquired a shipment of designer sportswear, it provoked an FBI investigation. The company bought 21,000 pairs of Calvin Klein, Gloria Vanderbilt, and Sassoon jeans, and widely advertised its coup: "These are the same jeans sold for $35 elsewhere, not discounter styles or close out," its advertisements read. "We purchased 21,000 pairs, and when they're gone there will be no more." The jeans reportedly sold out within hours at some stores and within a week across the entire 80-store chain. Klein, Vanderbilt, and Sassoon contacted federal authorities and sued Target, saying the goods must have been stolen—a charge the chain called "outrageous and irresponsible." Target said it got the apparel from a wholesaler it had done business with in the past, and the FBI backed off.[2] But the confrontation was symbolic—the first chink in the dam separating discounters from other retailers, and an indication of how much clout they had acquired in the marketplace. Ten years after suing Target for selling her jeans, Gloria Vanderbilt's tune had radically changed. In April 1989, the company was one of 12 advertisers who participated in a four-color, 16-page special advertising section in *USA Today*, promoting the grand opening of 30 former Gold Circle stores in the Southeast that Target acquired and remodeled. Even so, snaring department store brand names remained a daunting process. In a 1990 interview, Target president Gregg Steinhafel vowed that the store would "not back down" in finding "brands out there that will enhance our image as an upscale retailer."[3]

By 1999, Target had made significant inroads with respected labels, manufacturers who saw their customers gravitating to the discount store, and who recognized the financial benefits of doing business with a chain of more than 1,100 units. Target has become the mass-market outlet—in some cases the exclusive one—for manufacturers like Sony and Phillips Electronics, Calphalon cookware, Oneida silverware, Waverly home goods, Eddie Bauer camping gear, Stride Rite children's shoes, and Carter's Baby Tykes clothes. These firms recognize that their traditional venues—department stores—are stumbling badly, and their customers now favor discounters over other retail channels. (See Chapter 3.) "The wealthier group of people going to Target to buy their kitchen utensils and waste baskets and stuff and said, 'Wow, we can buy some fashion items here.' And this was happening at same time that consumers were saying they want value," explained Babson College Professor Michael Levy, coeditor of the *Journal of Retailing*. "Value doesn't mean cheap either—by definition, it's what you get for what you have to pay. A hard-core Neiman Marcus customer would say they get value for what they're paying. Having bought some really expensive cookware, I can tell you, what a waste. Target's cookware is a good value." At the same time it projects an upscale, high-fashion image, Target has been careful not to abandon its lower-income customers: When it began selling Calphalon priced at $199, for example, it also continued to market a $19.99 cookware set by Mirro.[4]

Tarzhay's upscale sensibility makes it acceptable for companies such as Calphalon to sell their goods in the store. Most customers don't realize the line is exclusive to Target, or might differ from the more costly collections offered elsewhere. In a mutually beneficial cycle, a manufacturer's appearance in Target adds to the chain's status. In October 2001, for example, Tupperware began selling its patented plastic products in Target. It was the American icon's first appearance in a retail chain since the 1940s, when Earl Tupper invented the spill-proof storage bins with the trademark "burp"—and made the world safe for leftovers. Tupperware sells from freestanding kiosks staffed by the infamous Tupperware party-throwers, who pitch home demonstrations while flogging their wares. Target provided "the same panache of our brand positioning," explained Tupperware chairman and CEO Rick Goings. "They are really at the top of the list when people are talking about where to register for bridal gifts right now—so it's the right kind of product with the right kind of retail environment."

Goings said Target's internal surveys show Tupperware is one of the most respected brands not only in its category, but also among all home furnishing products. "I think they are looking for brands that really draw people into the Target stores," Goings noted. "If you compare them to some other retailers, they have a fairly narrow product line that they show in any category in Target, but it's usually brands or product categories where there's a panache to it, or a design element. We match that, and that's what they've expressed to us. We've had many other retail chains who would like Tupperware products—from department stores to grocery chains to discounters—but we've basically told them no, we're going to make this work and grow with Target." Wouldn't a chic department store be a better match for Tupperware? "The distribution channel that is so much at risk today and having so much turmoil is the classic department store," Goings replied. "If we were selling Tupperware with kiosks in a department store, we'd be somewhere up on the second floor in the housewares department. You just don't get the foot traffic. And that isn't what you find in a Target or a SuperTarget store, so yes, things have really changed."

THE TARGETEERS

Target also manufactures its own goods through private labels such as Merona, Furio, Xhilaration, and in its groceries, Archer Farms. The company has an internal crew of trend spotters, or Targeteers, who scour the globe looking for the next hot color, shape, or material to distinguish the season's clothing, home décor, and other private label products. This practice dates back to 1990, and Target former merchandising executive Warren Feldman, a Bloomingdale's veteran. "A real merchant is out there being a part of his or her culture," Feldberg told an interviewer. "Two of the biggest things I learned at Bloomingdale's was a sense of creativity in product development, looking at the world as our shopping basket and finding ways to bring that basket to the average customer."[5]

In addition, Target's buyers benefit directly from their relationship with the company's department stores, another rationale for the corporation to keep them, despite shrinking sales. According to Target's former chairman and chief executive Floyd Hall, the relationship between Target buyers and the department stores has always been "a big one—the buyer in the discount store was seeing trends in fashion and colors coming out of the department store, and looking at what customers wealthier than his are buying, and then trying to develop that particular market." According to a *Harvard Business Review* study, Target's managers "learn about fashion trends much sooner than competitors by paying attention to the upscale retailers, whose buyers spot trends early through their contacts with leading fashion designers. For example, Target got wind of the (1999) 'gray craze' from other Dayton Hudson managers and tailored its apparel and home furnishings accordingly."[6] This sharing of fashion trends was reinforced when Robert Ulrich became chairman and CEO in 1994. (See Chapter 6.) Moreover, Target's buyers are highly trained and occupy a premier position in the company, Hall noted. "The merchandising organization at Target had a mentality, and has it today, that if you were the best buyer in the country at a department store you could come into Target as an *assistant* buyer," he explained. "They put the absolute best people they could find anywhere into it. If you did come in and want to be a buyer, you had to go through the hoops as an assistant buyer and do that for a number of years. You had strong incentive to become a buyer because the buyers are paid extremely well."

To help produce its private label goods, in 1998 Target Corporation bought Associated Merchandising Corporation (AMC), which sources vendors and contractors overseas. But Target has been producing private label for years, starting with health and beauty products back in the 1970s. At the time, it formulated a strict quality standard: The private label had to be the same quality as the leading brand at a cheaper price, or better than the leading brand at the same price. Meanwhile, because it orders in huge volume, Target can obtain higher grades of fabric and quality construction for its private label goods. Target also thinks carefully about how to merchandise high-end lines. The first nine items from Sony, introduced in summer 2002, were exclusives designed for a female consumer; Target decided the most effective way to reach that audience was to put them in home décor, rather than electronics.[7] On the Target website, there is a direct link to Sony's "boutique."

JOHN PELLEGRENE

For more than a decade, Target's creative heart has been John Pellegrene, the former head of marketing who retired in 2001, but still consults for the company. Pellegrene is another Dayton's veteran who joined the firm in 1969, and spent years honing his experience on the department store side before moving to Target in 1988. A snappy dresser and visionary thinker, Pellegrene was responsible for some of Target's greatest hits over the last decade: The Michael Graves collaboration, the funky, award-winning bull's-eye advertising campaigns, the Club Wedd bridal registry program, the Take Charge of Education credit card initiative. In one interview, he described his mission as "always bringing something new to the party," and his motto as: "Solve problems—don't create them."[8]

Former coworkers describe him as versatile, quick-witted, good humored, kind and prolific, moving easily from marketing to merchandising to advertising. "He has a knack for pizzazz—he connects the dots in ways others can't," said Jeff Turner, former creative director for Marshall Field and Company. "You end up with this enormous, creative, noisy marketing program." Turner recalled the way Pellegrene keyed in on ice skating, for example, partnering with Scott Hamilton to sponsor "Stars on Ice" just before the sport took off. One ad executive said Pellegrene could have easily been chairman of a major retailer—and he himself told *Brandweek* he'd be a college professor if he wasn't in marketing—but preferred not to sacrifice time with his five children.[9] Said one collaborator simply: "I revere John Pellegrene."

Insiders say Pellegrene's successor, Michael Francis, is cut from the same cloth—another out-of-the-box thinker who started with the company and rose through the ranks on the department store side. A former colleague described the time Francis created a European flea market in Marshall Field's, sending a team of buyers to the Marché aux Puces in Paris where they bought millions of dollars of merchandise. They filled the 8th floor auditorium in Minneapolis for a three-day event, and then took everything on the road to Chicago for a second sale, attracting the kind of excited crowds that pushed overall store sales through the roof.

Pellegrene and Francis have cultivated a network of freelance consultants who help keep the company on-trend. Mark Sotnick, a former media producer who has worked with Meryl Streep and the pianist George Winston, collaborated with Pellegrene on a Christmas promotion years ago. As an independent consultant, Sotnick's current task is to steer intriguing ideas and creative personalities Target's way. In one case, he found a unique nursery in Rhode Island whose owner advises Target on its gardening department. On another occasion, he introduced the chain to a personable chef, Ming Tsai of Blue Ginger restaurant in Massachusetts, who designed an Asian-inspired cookware line. "They look to people who instinctively make trends, as opposed to following them, to help them stay ahead of the curve," Sotnick said. "Target is not afraid of ideas. What's important is their willingness to go outside looking for ideas—ideas from anywhere are good." This search for ideas was also born of necessity, he added: "When Target first started, they couldn't get the brands. So they created their own brands. What was their weakness became their strength. They're smarter than hell."

CULTIVATING AUTHENTIC DESIGN

Pellegrene and Francis have doggedly expanded Target brands through off-beat licensing deals with a wide range of designers, whose names may not ring a bell in middle America, but are clearly respected artists. They include the architect Michael Graves, celebrity makeup artist Sonia Kashuk, designers Mossimo Giannulli, Todd Oldham, Stephen Sprouse, Mark Ecko, Philippe Starck, Liz Lange and Cynthia Rowley (my cousin), who is designing home products with a partner under the label "Swell by Cynthia Rowley and Ilene Rosenzweig." Target works in tandem with the designers to develop products that can be manufactured at a suitable price point for the chain's customers. "I think Target does two things," said Cynthia Cohen, founder, Strategic Mindshare, a California retail consulting firm. "They make trends—taking a lesser-known designer but still quality designer, and having him design toasters is making their own trend. On the other hand they are a follower—when trendspotters identify it, they want to come just after, just before it gets to the masses. Target can't be too early—you've got to be in the belly of the bell-shaped curve, not the skinny end." In other words, leading edge, not bleeding edge.

The Swell Brand: Doing a Deal with Target

When I was asked if I'd be interested in writing a book on the Target Corporation, I was immediately intrigued. Not only was I a fan of the store, I also had a smidgen of experience in the fashion industry: In the late 1980s, I worked for my cousin, Cynthia Rowley, a designer on Seventh Avenue. (We grew up together in Illinois. There were eleven kids in my family, and she was pals with one of my sisters. When I arrived in New York and called her up, she confessed later, she wasn't sure which Rowley I was. Later she would call me the sister she never had. I called her the *fifth* sister I never had.)

At the time, there were just four of us in the company doing everything—ordering fabric, cutting samples, selling the line, working with the fashion press, vacuuming the showroom—and I found the garment center a much tougher pasture than journalism, to which I returned a year later. I ended up at CNN business news as an on-air producer; Cynthia, an enormously creative talent and brilliant businesswoman, went on to build an international empire that included women's wear, men's wear, a dozen different licenses for everything from shoes to make-up, and a chain of retail stores, among other projects. More recently, she had written a best-selling book, *Swell: A Girl's Guide to the Good Life,* with her friend Ilene Rosenzweig, a former style editor at the *New York Times.* That led to a deal with ABC and Imagine Films for a sitcom based on their adventures in New York. When I called her up to say I was writing a book about Target, there was a long silence on the line. "I'm doing something with Target too," she replied. As it turned out, she and Ilene had negotiated a three-year deal to design a line of home products under the Swell brand. I was genuinely surprised. That Cynthia was designing for Target and I was writing a book about the store is an unbelievable coincidence.

Admittedly, it's a little unorthodox to interview a relative you've known all your life for a journalistic endeavor. But Cynthia agreed to speak with me about the Swell collection and share insights into Target. Here are the highlights of our interview:

Q: What designs will be offered under the Swell brand?

A: Home products, lifestyle products, bedding, bath, tabletop— dishes, glasses, tablecloths, napkins, all that stuff; we have a

24-foot run of bedding. We have long-term contract—three years plus—so we're going to slowly add things, pet products, toys. Really cool prints and patterns are important in defining the brand—it's all meant to have a fun, playful quality. We're trying to be inventive with things because they can make so many pieces of an item.

Q: Give me some examples.

A: We're doing a round beach towel, so you don't have to move the towel, you just spin yourself around when the sun moves. You know how people put charms on wine glasses to keep track of their glass? We thought it would be funny to put numbers on cocktail glasses, because you can also use them to keep track of how many cocktails you've had. We invented waterproof gift bags so you can bring flowers to somebody and have water in the bag. We made decorative trash bags for parties with really cool prints on them. We tried to mix traditional things with kind of fun, special things; they're classic, but the packaging and marketing and the way they work in your home is not classic.

Q: Why did you want to work with Target?

A: I wanted to do home products. I dabbled in doing dishes with another company, and doing sheets with another company, but it was all sort of piecemeal, and it's so much harder to control all these different companies and relationships. If I did dishes with one person, bedding with someone else, and something else with someone else, it could be in all different stores, all different places, all different prices, really hard to control. So the best way to do it was with one retailer that could oversee a whole lifestyle brand. Target is known for their marketing and merchandising, and to be able to house it all together under one roof is really the ideal situation.

Q: How did you originally connect with Target?

A: I met one of their advertising consultants at a party. He said, "I've been mocking up ads for Target with your stuff for years. You'd never do anything with them would you?" And I said, "No, not really." I just couldn't see how I could do fashion for them. But then the *Swell* book took on a life of its own, and we developed this brand, which really seemed to appeal to a wider audience. As the book sold, we got the idea of doing Swell TV, and then thought the perfect tie-in would be to have product on the show. I thought this was a way to maximize all the other projects we're doing.

Q: Why not go with Wal-Mart, which is so much bigger than Target?

A: They have no style. Target has a spirit. When you walk in the store, it's bright, upbeat, positive, optimistic, inspired. It's definitely the image of what it means to have a happy shopping experience. Target is the leader, they've been the leader in this whole philosophy of great design for the masses. It's just their own thing, and they're going right to the sources to get great design.

Q: What do you think of Target's advertising?

A: It's one message: It's the image of the store, but they really do try to keep the integrity of each individual brand. So (Philippe) Starck was really Starck, and Todd (Oldham) was Todd, but it also had that overall Target kind of feeling. After talking to them for a long, long time, I realize that they really try to nurture talent and nurture creativity and really try not to have any influence on the actual product, as long as it's well-designed and offers value to their customer.

Q: A lot of the designers who have signed on with Target talk about their desire to make fashion more democratic. Is that your goal?

A: I don't think it's necessarily making fashion democratic. I think fashion will always be something that's very aspirational. And for me, I'm going to continue to do the high-end fashion and do the more democratic lifestyle/home stuff. I think it's more the way people live. Everyone wants to look great and sexy and cool, and clothes like that can make you feel really good. But I don't think people feel the same way about their home. The way we're trying to do home stuff is more irreverent and more disposable. I've always bought all my stuff at garage sales for three dollars so I have that sort of disposable mentality.

Q: Who does the manufacturing, production, and quality control?

A: They partner you with different vendors who they think are best for your brand, they give them the program per se, and then we work with them directly to get them all the information, all the specs and technical things. We check the quality of the samples and the quality of production. The thing with Target is that the manufacturers make up so much money in the volume, they can offer much better quality.

Q: How often do you meet with them?

A: We have meetings once a week with the New York liaison and then we go to Minneapolis once a month.

Q: So from the time you start designing, how long does it take to actually produce a collection?

A: Six to eight months I would say. It's pretty fast.

Q: Was it lucrative?

A: It's good, it definitely has a lot of restrictions so that it can only be *so* good. I probably just said too much.

Q: Did the philanthropic aspect of their business have any bearing on your decision to work with them?

A: Yes. It's pretty amazing that they give away $2 million a week to philanthropic causes. I'm trying to do that with our advertising now; so instead of putting up a billboard that's just a billboard, I'd rather have it be a park bench that's going to help the community.

Q: Do you think you'll reach a new audience through Target?

A: Definitely. I felt I was starting to reach them with my cosmetics line, which is more mass (market). Then the books were even more democratic. The next step, once you have the audience for the books, is to give them something accessible, and so Target was perfect. I think fashion is a different audience.

Q: If Target didn't exist, would you have done a line for mass retail?

A: If they didn't exist, I guess we'd have to start opening Swell stores.

That's not to say the company hasn't stumbled—dramatically in at least one case—over that edge. In August 2002, Target pulled from all of its stores shorts and baseball caps marked with an "88"—code among neo-Nazis for "Heil Hitler," because H is the eighth letter of the alphabet. The store was alerted to the problem by a California shopper and the Southern Poverty Law Center, a national organization that tracks racist groups. Joseph Rodriguez, a 51-year-old video producer/director at the University of California-Davis, was shopping in a Sacramento-area Target store when he noticed a pair of red shorts covered with skulls and other symbols, and the number 88. "I just thought they were cool," said Rodriguez in a statement issued by the Southern Poverty Law Center. "But when I saw the '88' I couldn't believe it."[10] Rodriguez knew of the significance of the "88" from watching a documentary about white supremacist music. Mark Potok of the Southern Poverty Law Center said neo-Nazis often use symbols or codes "as a way of communicating with each other under the radar screen of the public. The noxious thing is when these symbols make their way into popular culture and gain widespread acceptance in the mainstream," he told Reuters. For its part, Target said it was investigating how the style, made by its private label line, Utility, got approved. "Target is a family-oriented store and company and it is not our intent to carry any merchandise that promotes hate," the company said in a statement.

The Utility incident aside, Target's more successful design alliances differ widely from the approach at Wal-Mart, which taps celebrities like Mary-Kate and Ashley Olson to license their names to products designed by an anonymous manufacturer. Target's decision to work with lesser-known personalities but real innovators also squares with its long-time philosophy of making the store itself—not the names or products it carries—the true brand. More than a decade ago, Pellegrene told a reporter: "To market Wal-Mart is a price. To market Target is a nuance, which is much more delicate. You have to communicate that you have design, trends and silhouettes—basically, that you're the Bloomingdale's of the discount industry."[11] In 2002, Francis told the *Wall Street Journal* the chain has no plan to create individual, in-store boutiques for its designers: "Target is the brand, and we're not going to be a mini-mall."[12] Shoppers come to Target not knowing precisely what they'll discover, but expecting to find excitement and inspiration among its collections. Dallas Target fan Melodie Layman typically spends two hours exploring. "What happens is you start looking and it's, 'Oh that's cute, oh that's cute!' I always putz around for an hour getting stuff I half need and half don't need, but I always end up with something I shouldn't have bought." Target's emphasis on making the retailer itself synonymous with original design also contrasts strongly with the direction taken by Kmart in its mega-deal with Martha Stewart: The doyenne of domesticity is unquestionably the brand name—and Kmart merely the outlet. Moreover, Kmart found out the hard way that making a store synonymous with a dominant brand can backfire, after Stewart's reputation was smudged by negative publicity surrounding the insider trading investigation into biotech firm Imclone.

THE GRAVES PHENOMENON

Target's major foray into cutting-edge design started in 1999 with Princeton, New Jersey architect Michael Graves. A winner of numerous architectural awards, Graves has produced an impressive body of international work over the years that includes hotels, shops and restaurants at Walt Disney World; libraries and cultural institutions; sports and recreation facilities, offices and theaters. He also designs whimsical and distinctive products such as furniture, textiles, lighting fixtures, consumer goods, and accessories. In 1998, Graves received a commission to build scaffolding and a temporary cover for the Washington Monument during its massive overhaul, which included repairing some cracks the length of a Greyhound bus. Graves created tubular, aluminum scaffolding and wrapped it in a 55-story slipcover made of blue and gray translucent fabric, with a grid-like pattern imitating the mortar and stone surface of the monument itself. Powerful lights gave the "slipcover" a spectacular glow at night.[13] The Park Service commissioned the project in conjunction with Target, a major benefactor of the restoration. When Michael Graves met Target's Pellegrene, a monumental partnership, so to speak, was born. Consultant Mark Sotnick said the Graves deal underscores Target's creativity. "A lot of things Pellegrene did in hindsight look obvious," he noted. "But at the time— Michael Graves? Why in the world would a discount store be doing something with a fancy architect that the masses certainly don't know?"

A year after Graves and Target officials met, the first 300 items by the architect—sleek home décor, kitchen utensils, and small appliances—appeared on Target's shelves. They reportedly met with only moderate success at first, but Target stood by the Graves collection as a critical part of its differentiation strategy. As the architect expanded his creations into casual tabletop, kitchen utensils, home décor and home furnishings, sales began to rise.[14] Target soon began to display his work next to an artsy black-and-white photo and description of the architect. Graves may eventually take Target design to a larger venue: According to the *New York Times*, in November 2002, he was working on developing a prefab house for the retailer.[15]

YOUTH, BEAUTY, AND MAGIC: MORE HIGH-QUALITY ALLIANCES

The success of the Graves partnership pushed the chain into hyperdrive: Target began rolling out high-quality design alliances in quick succession. It placed a big bet on Mossimo Giannulli, a California designer who got his start selling T-shirts from his car. Giannulli manufactured trendy sportswear under his own label for 13 years, but sales had waned. Target provided a three-year guarantee of $1 billion in cumulative sales for its use of Mossimo designs and its trademark, according to a report by research firm William Blair.[16] Target contracted to pay at least $27 million in royalties over three years if the product met minimum sales goals—a royalty fee of just 2.7 percent of sales. Target is known to be a tough negotiator: As part of the deal, Mossimo had to close company-owned stores in California, slash its workforce, terminate production contracts, and end virtually all relationships with customers, including the department store Dillards, which had been responsible for more than 40 percent of its sales.[17] Mossimo's clothing lines have been well received, and fans are agog at the values. "You know that black Mossimo dress that's in all the magazine ads? I *want* that dress," said Amy Merrick, a *Wall Street Journal* reporter who covers the company, referring to a short, backless summer sheath featured widely in Target's promotions. "It's a $20 dress, and I'm actually excited that it's going to be at Target next month so I can buy it."

Target followed up with other partnerships—an exclusive line of beauty products from celebrity makeup artist Sonia Kashuk, and a deal for home furnishings from fashion designer Todd Oldham. Earlier in his career, Oldham, renowned for his lush colors and playful, elaborate prints, showed $5,000 couture creations on runway models like Cindy Crawford, while Julia Roberts and other stars kept the paparazzi busy in the front row. He was also a regular on MTV's "House of Style." In 1998, Oldham sold his trademark to Jones Apparel Group, and in 2001, signed on to design a collection called "Dorm Room" for Target. It featured collegiate-themed bedding, lamps, chairs, kitchen utensils, and decorative pillows in retro patterns and shades. A maroon bed rest sports bright orange piping; teal-colored waste baskets are stenciled with the word "trashed"; boldly striped jersey knit bedding reverses to a solid pattern splashed with colorful stars; pillows in corduroy, felt and sequins retailed for $7 a pop. "Target and I have very similar views about what's important in design," Oldham said in a statement. "We both believe that consumers crave design that's smart and interesting, while at the same time is accessible and affordable."[18] Oldham was featured in television commercials that emphasized his image, which, like Target's, is both hip and clean-cut—Target's ads referred to him as "boy wonder of the fashion world." Target followed up quickly with another high profile alliance: Marc Ecko, a former graffiti artist and hip-hop-inspired designer, introduced his Physical Science collection of casual wear for men and boys. Ecko declared himself "an avid Target shopper for years."[19]

Next, the cheerful Midwestern chain struck an unlikely alliance with Stephen Sprouse, a fashion outlaw and longtime fixture on the downtown Manhattan scene. A friend of Sonia Kashuk, Sprouse ran a business that flourished and slumped numerous times over the years. He has dressed Courtney Love, David Bowie, Iggy Pop, and Blondie's Deborah Harry in her band's heyday, and is known for his irreverent looks. Sprouse, who also dabbles in art, video and technology, created the must-have graffiti-covered handbag for Louis Vuitton in 2001, which retailed for more than $500. The next summer, under the "Americaland" label, he designed red, white, and blue clothing—including a fetching $6.99 T-shirt, as well as affordable picnic supplies, beach umbrellas, and skateboards for Target. Target said the collection brought Sprouse's "in-your-face patriotic vision" to shoppers; Sprouse, in typical bad-boy fashion, apparently supplied no comment for the press release.[20]

But Target wasn't finished pushing the envelope. The company cut a wide licensing agreement with Philippe Starck, the wacky Parisian best known for his stylized hotel interiors, including the Royalton, Paramount and Hudson in New York; hip bars like Café Costes in Paris; stores and restaurants in Hong Kong, Japan, and London. For Target he created Starck Reality, a collection of home, office, kitchen, bath, and baby products (including a jewel-trimmed baby monitor that mom can string around her neck). Target highlighted the importance of the Starck alliance by holding the collection's debut at the influential Milan Furniture Fair. "Working with Target has helped me to fulfill a dream that I've held all my life," Starck said in a statement. "My goal in this democratization of design is to make possible the most joyful and exciting things and experiences for the maximum number of people. Today we don't need more design, more pretensions—we need more happiness and more magic available to everyone."[21]

For all the happy lip service to joy, magic, and affordable fashion by and for the people, these licensing partnerships provide an outlet—sometimes a highly lucrative one—for manufacturers and designers whose alternatives are shrinking. In 2001, for example, Target operated more than 1,050 discount stores and had about $34 billion in sales; Macy's, by comparison, had around 250 stores with $9 billion in revenues. With the dramatic changes in customer expectations, shopping habits, and the lack of stigma attached to Target in particular, the upscale vendors are now often the ones initiating contact with Target, instead of the other way around. "I know of other apparel manufacturers who are going directly to Target because they're not getting the volume through department stores anymore," noted Salomon Smith Barney analyst Weinswig. As Michael Francis chirped to the *Wall Street Journal*, "We get calls every week."[22]

And while it works with the hottest designers of the moment, Target is also busy identifying the creative talent of the future. In 1998, the company began sponsoring the "Target/CFDA Design Initiative," an internship competition for graduating seniors of the nation's top design schools. Applicants submit a design portfolio with an essay, and the winner receives a full-year paid gig with Target. Sang Ly, a graduate of the Otis College of Art & Design School, won the award in 2002. She says she was drawn to Target by its advertising. "They've gotten a lot of media attention and become innovative in the way they handle marketing," said Ly, chatting from Los Angeles in a pair of Target pajamas purchased with a $1,000 company gift certificate that was part of the prize. Ly, a native of Thailand who moved to L.A. with her parents at age three, relates to Target's cheap chic: "When I was a teenager I couldn't afford designer clothes, so I made things on my own." The program gives winners experience working with Target's internal design teams in women's, men's and children's wear. Ly said her winning collection of street clothes for girls—called "booboo"—was inspired by tennis stars Venus and Serena Williams and the female Olympic bobsled team.

Not all of Target's ventures bear fruit. Niki Taylor by Liz Claiborne, a women's clothing line that involved the blonde supermodel, was rolled out in 2001. But Taylor bailed out right as the collection went into stores. Target and Liz Claiborne came up with a substitute line—Meg Allen by Liz Claiborne—but it lacked the celebrity appeal of the original line.[23]

DELIVERING THE HUMAN TOUCH

Target has attracted hordes of devotees because its internal culture cares so deeply about creativity and design, and makes it a priority. "I talk to a lot of companies where they get really excited about expense control," said *Wall Street Journal* reporter Merrick. "But at Target they get really excited about the merchandise— 'Have you seen that, have you seen that? We're going to try this!' In their conference calls they're really detailed about all the new stuff they're trying. And they wouldn't be like that if new, creative merchandise weren't so important to them."

Consider the experience of Howard Ben Tré, a Rhode Island-based artist known for his massive cast glass sculpture. Ben Tré designed the plaza in front of Target's new headquarters in downtown Minneapolis, a tree-lined space featuring granite semi-circular benches, sculpture, a fountain, and lit pavers to create a communal corner on the pedestrian mall. "I have a lot of different clients and they may like what I do, but they're never willing to put me on as high a plane as they are," Ben Tré said. "I mean these guys make a lot of money. Target's a huge corporation. Usually you go in for a presentation like that, you're a little intimidated. So I go and make my presentation—and [CEO] Bob Ulrich turns to John Pellegrene and says, 'This guy is a genius!' It kind of blew my mind. He wasn't grudgingly saying, 'You know I think this is a good idea'—he was *so* enthusiastic. It really set the tone."

Whether it's a Michael Graves tea kettle, a little black dress by Mossimo, or a neon-hued bed-in-a-bag by Todd Oldham, Target's products "become supermodels of the company," argued branding expert Marc Gobé. "Customization gets people's attention. If you can feel the hand of the designer—anything that takes you away from machine-made—that's moving away from the commoditization you find at Kmart. Target delivers the human touch through communication, through their products, through the design of their stores and their people. You feel that personal touch and feel reassured in a world that's not reassuring." In the next chapter, we take a look at fundamental shifts in retailing, media, and technology that helped pave the way for Target's success.

⊙ CHECK OUT

The Right Stuff

Designer brands made affordable: Target collaborates with leading companies such as Sony and Calphalon to develop exclusive, affordable collections specifically for the discounter. Customers recognize the name and aren't necessarily aware the product is different from the manufacturer's more upscale lines, adding to Target's cachet.

Cutting-edge private label goods: Target looks far and wide for new ideas, using its own globe-trotting trendspotters, gathering intelligence from the company's Marshall Field department store buyers, and employing a network of external consultants to keep it on trend. Target's buyers are highly trained and well-compensated. The chain has historically held private label goods to a strict quality standard, enhancing its own brand. Because it orders goods in such high volume, Target has the clout to obtain higher grades of fabric and better-quality construction.

Licensing deals: Target's differentiation strategy seeks ideas outside the mainstream and uses licensing agreements to make its own trends, for example, a well-respected architect designing small appliances and housewares. Target chooses innovative but lesser-known artists (rather than celebrities) to create unique merchandise at an acceptable price point. As a result, products feel like custom designs rather than commodities.

Unique branding strategy: Target brings together a variety of manufacturers and designers to create broad, sophisticated and high-quality assortments, but it also subordinates these names to its own; the company markets Target as the brand, rather than the individual products or name brands it carries.

CHAPTER 3

Inside the Mind of the Bargain Hunter

In my next life I would love to be a cashier
at Target, scanning all that merchandise,
wearing my red shirt and khaki pants.

—Tory Johnson, business owner,
Target fanatic

"HOW CAN YOU GET HURT?"

It's Saturday afternoon in Fairfield, New Jersey, and 31-year-old Bob Dzienis is on a mission. Crisp and casual in jeans and a white button-down shirt, he hops into his beloved hunter green Volkswagen Golf—the four-door hatchback made famous in the "Da-da-da" commercial of the late 1990s—and roars out of the driveway of the two-family home where he rents the upstairs unit. New Jersey's twisted highways, with their sparse signage, random local and express lanes, and bizarre U-turns, can stupefy the amateur. But Dzienis grew up in nearby Parsippany and he knows these roads like the back of his hand.

Dzienis cruises south on the Garden State Parkway, a cool Benjamin burning a hole in his wallet, and makes his way to Route 22—a congested, four-lane thoroughfare lousy with strip malls and car dealerships. Another 20 minutes of aggressive zigzagging around SUVs, and he arrives at his destination, a Target Greatland in Union. He heads straight for the men's section. "I really like their Mossimo collection because I'd seen that in surfing shops. I remember seeing it at Target and thinking wow, they sell Mossimo," he said. "I found a belt once that seriously looked like you could get at Banana Republic for $40 and I only paid $5. That, and an awesome turtleneck merino wool sweater that I could have paid $60 for elsewhere and I think I only paid $12. My signature phrase is, 'How can you get hurt?' You pay $5 for a belt, how can you get hurt?"

Actually, the ones feeling the pain are full-price retailers, being left in the dust by millions of Bob Dzienis's. While Target has been masterful in luring shoppers into its stores, there is no denying that part of its ascendance is due to a dramatic shift in the retailing environment, media, and technology. The 1990s saw a creeping democracy in fashion—a merger of mass and class—from grunge and vintage to dress-down Fridays to soccer moms. Instead of trickling down from the wealthy, fashion trends began to trickle up from the street, with many designers taking their cues from the hip-hop style of the inner city. As the boom and excess of the 1980s collapsed into bust and recession in the early 1990s, it became sexy to find a good deal. "Sharon Stone at the Oscars wearing a black turtle neck from The Gap was a signal that it was okay to buy bargain, and you could look great," said Cindi Leive, editor-in-chief of *Glamour* magazine. "There's no longer a feeling that it's déclassé to find something great and cheap. Among certain upper-middle class shoppers it's tongue in cheek—'Look at us slumming at Wal-Mart.'" Witness Sarah Jessica Parker, a fashion icon in her role in "Sex and the City," gushing about her frilly, comfy, $12.99 Target pajamas to talk show host Conan O'Brien. Or Camryn Manheim, winner of the 1998 Emmy for her role in "The Practice" ("This is for all the big girls!"), sporting Target earrings to the awards show.

The insular world of the runway show, once an exclusive club of store buyers and fashion editors, became a media spectacle—MTV, E!, and a variety of new style channels turned designers into rock stars while spreading fashion to the masses. *In Style*, one of the most successful magazine launches in decades, showcased celebrity attire and home design in a glamorous yet utterly accessible way. "You look at *In Style* and Gwyneth Paltrow is wearing Marc Jacobs and Versace," said Atlanta graphic designer and Target fan Stephanie Sonnenfeld. "I love that stuff, but I don't make tons of money. But you can go to Target and Nordstrom Rack and TJ Maxx and make your own little Gwyneth Paltrow-esque thing, and get the look of what you see in *In Style* and *W*. There's also a psychological high, thinking, 'I got this for $5 when someone else paid $50.'" Even the couture bibles of the trust fund set, *Vogue* and

Harper's Bazaar, began offering fairly regular features showing how to "get the look for less"—once the preserve of their sister magazines aimed at working girls.

RETAIL MAYHEM

At the same time that low-priced fashion was becoming socially acceptable, even smart, there was suddenly a preponderance of it across the nation's retail landscape: warehouse clubs, supercenters, outlet malls; "category killers" such as Bed Bath & Beyond; high-style European chains including Ikea and H & M; and websites like Bluefly.com, which boast substantial discounts on Prada, Donna Karan, and Calvin Klein. "It used to be when you really wanted a great deal on something, you'd have to go to Loehmann's and be weeding through the junk for hours, or you'd drive to an outlet mall an hour and a half from your house," said *Glamour's* Leive. "When I look at some of the stores now, I think, where was that stuff when I was 22 and making $16,000 a year? There just used to be a much larger gap—this Grand Canyon of space between designer and cheap—and that gap has been closed." (Even Loehmann's has been swamped by the competition; it filed for Chapter 11 bankruptcy protection in 1999.)

Part of the gap has been closed by technology. Sophisticated information systems have made the supply chain more efficient, so goods get to stores faster. The Internet in particular helped no-name manufacturers knock off designer looks and get them on the racks in the same season as the originals. (And in some cases, the discount goods are being made in the same overseas factories as the designer goods; depending on the volume produced, sometimes the fabric is a higher grade.) Better information and distribution networks help the discounters keep the hottest goods in stock. As the quality, selection, and availability of discount goods have expanded, millions of consumers have wised up to the fact that they don't have to pay full price, and the stigma attached to discount shopping has faded. Those trends have given rise to a fierce breed of retailing connoisseur: the bargain hunters. Once left to brawl with their own kind over end-of-the-season scraps at Bloomie's, or forage through the overstuffed racks of Marshall's or Filene's Basement, the bargain hunters have overrun the retail landscape, declaring they're not going to take it anymore. The search for value appears to be a fundamental shift rather than a cyclical trend: Throughout the latter half of the 1990s, even as the economy boomed, discounters continued to grab market share.

These modern-day Monty Halls admit to getting a psychological high from making a deal. Shopping is a game of strategy, where the goal is to outsmart the prey (or those preying on your wallet). Tory Johnson, owner of a Manhattan recruiting firm and self-proclaimed Target fanatic who can afford to shop anywhere, put it this way: "Whether we make a lot of money or don't, we all work really, really hard. There's a sense of pride to be able to say, 'I saved money.' I don't think it has the appearance of being cheap. I think it's a badge of honor to say, 'I'm a smart, savvy shopper, I know where to get great deals.' "

Another facet of the bargain hunter's psychology is the triumph of the high school pauper who couldn't afford a proper Izod shirt, showing up at his reunion in high style. "[When I get a deal] I feel good, I feel more confident," said Dzienis. "I think working, paying the rent, doing those types of things, you just realize you don't need big brand names. You can still find things that are made well and they are a good price. I take my Target turtleneck and my $9.99 Banana Republic pants and my $7 shoes and people are like,

'Wow that's a great outfit.' No one knows what my labels are—that's fine, I'm happy with the way I look."

Massachusetts teacher and Target shopper Stephanie Dines agreed: "I'd have to say once I got married and we started to be a little more careful about our income and save for our house, that's when I stopped caring about whether certain things were name brand. I was more concerned with finding something that fit me, and that I liked. Once I started realizing I could buy pants for $70 at [The] Limited or get them at Marshall's for $29, and it was close enough in style, there was no reason to buy the brand. The change for me [was] that I could find things at discount stores; [in the past] you either had to wait a year, and it wasn't close to the same quality."

Research shows more consumers feel the way Dzienis and Dines do about labels. According to Brand Keys, a New York City marketing research firm, the importance of logos, labels, and trademarks has fallen significantly. When asked how important apparel brand logos and labels are to consumers now versus a few years ago, 57 percent of those interviewed said they are now less important. Of 7,500 respondents, almost six times as many said logos and labels were now either "much less" or "less" important to them, versus those who said they were now "much more" or "more" important. "Increasingly apparel brands do not resonate with the values of their target consumers," said Robert Passikoff, president of Brand Keys. Older consumers were most vociferous in rejecting designer labels. Some 69 percent of those age 45 to 59 said their importance had declined—an ominous sign, given the swelling ranks of baby boomers. But even among the youngest demographic, age 21 to 34, over twice as many respondents said logos and labels are now less important. "It appears that even among traditionally fashion-conscious younger adults, a rejection of the use of one's clothes as a statement about oneself seems to be taking place," said Passikoff.

What does seem to matter is value. In retail-speak, the trend of feeding up and down the fashion food chain is known as "cross-shopping." "It means that a shopper may go to Bergdorf Good-man and buy an Armani jacket and pair it with a $20 tank top or a $30 pair of jeans from somewhere else," said Professor Bart Weitz, executive director of the Miller Center for Retailing Educa-tion and Research at the University of Florida, Gainesville, Florida. "For fashion accessories where people are able to see and feel the difference, people are still willing to pay a lot of money. For things they can't, they say 'Why bother?' People aren't buying new wardrobes every year the way they used to. They either buy some-thing fashionable that won't last or classical designs."

That describes Patti O'Donnell perfectly. The founder of a Chicago public relations firm, she enjoys the guilt-free allure of Target's disposable fashion. "I love buying clothes there—espe-cially summer stuff, because I can wear it out and then donate it to a charity. I'm a conservative dresser by nature, and Target is be-coming more stylish. If I can get a season out of [a shirt] for ten bucks that's great, and if it's only fashionable for one season, I don't feel guilty because I'm not spending a lot of money." Her other clothes, by contrast, are an investment. "I have a Nicole Miller black dress that was expensive, but it was classic and I knew it would never go out of style. I've worn it to every wedding for the last seven years," she joked.

Many Target shoppers like O'Donnell say they didn't go to Tar-get looking for fashion. It was more a funny thing that happened on the way to the pots and pans. "I am a Target junkie," said 29-year-old Liz Novak of Rochester, New York, who raves about the $10 Mossimo tees she buys over and over in different colors to wear under work suits. She shops twice a month and spends $100 a pop on her Target credit card. "I used to buy only housewares at Target, but a few months ago I wandered into their clothing section and was hooked. I no longer shop at department stores, unless they have some huge half-off sale."

THE SAKS SHOPPER SNUBBED

Those huge half-off sales are no accident. In response to the discounters, upscale stores began holding promotions earlier and earlier in the season, launching a continual price war, and virtually training consumers to wait for a bargain. Over the years, in an effort to cut costs, they reduced the number of salespeople on the floor—eliminating a key factor that distinguished them from discounters. The Byzantine layout of department stores, designed for an era when women could spend a full day browsing and lunching, became a turnoff to time-starved working parents seeking close-in parking and a speedy checkout. Department stores also suffered from a cloned sheep problem—with the same designer boutiques carrying the same items, the stores all looked alike. Stock that failed to sell in department stores often wound up in off-price chains, further encouraging shoppers to avoid paying full price. As a result of all of these trends, department stores' share of the apparel market fell to 40 percent in 2001 from 70 percent two decades ago; its portion of furniture sales is down to 5 percent from 40 percent, according to Service Industry Research Systems, a market research firm in Highland Heights, Kentucky. Salomon Smith Barney retail analyst Deborah Weinswig said, "I don't want to go as far as saying department stores are dead, but I was talking to someone in my office about picking up something at Saks, and they almost turned up their nose at me and said, 'You shop at department stores?' I said, 'It's around the corner, where else am I going to go?' I never thought I would have to defend shopping at Saks. People feel they've been taken advantage of. At Costco it's $22.99 for Polo Ralph Lauren jeans—a third of what it would cost me at a department store. It's cool to be frugal."

Branding expert Marc Gobé said Target clearly made a conscious decision long ago that set the stage for its success today. "I think that Target could not have accomplished what it accomplished unless a group of people within Target decided they would bring to America a level of affordable products but with style. They have the culture, but also had the vision." In the next chapter, we'll look at how Target expresses that vision through its award-winning advertising and promotions.

⊙ CHECK OUT

Inside the Mind of the Bargain Hunter

Multiple retail channels: A variety of new retailing concepts have appeared over the last two decades, including warehouse clubs, supercenters, outlet malls, websites, "category killers" (such as Bed, Bath & Beyond) and high-style, affordable European chains. As a result, shoppers are reluctant to pay full price, and lacking time, tend to favor the most convenient retail channels.

Technology: Sophisticated information systems and distribution networks have made the supply chain more efficient, so hot looks hit Target at the same time as upscale retailers, and stay in stock.

Cross-shopping and cheap chic: As the timing and quality of discounters' products have improved, shoppers are more likely to pair an inexpensive piece with a luxurious one. Whether in home furnishings or clothing, consumers now tend to buy classics that last for years and pair them with seasonal, disposable trend items.

Media: High fashion has become more accessible in recent years as television and magazines put a heavier focus on celebrity style. At the same time, more media began focusing on getting the look for less.

Social attitudes: The stigma attached to discount stores has faded; shoppers who find deals think of themselves as smart and savvy rather than cheap. Studies show labels and logos are losing their influence.

CHAPTER 4

Advertising and Promotion

The simple iconography of that little
bull's-eye—it's ingenious. The logo
says "we get it."

—Bill Oberlander, senior partner/executive
creative director, Ogilvy & Mather

THE OUT-OF-TOWNERS

When Target arrived on the East Coast in the mid-1990s, it had a scuffle with one of its advertising firms, Kirshenbaum Bond & Partners. The agency devised a cryptic print ad to promote the opening of the first New York-area Target store. It featured the bull's-eye logo with the line: "If you know what this symbol means . . . call 888-100-1235." Target wanted to put its name at the bottom of the ad. Knowing the average New Yorker's obsessive lust to be in the know, the agency argued against it. "We said, just run the bull's-eye, and people who know the brand will get it, and people who don't know the brand will want to know what it's all about," said Bill Oberlander, former creative director with Kirshenbaum, who is now senior partner/executive creative director with Ogilvy & Mather. "They said, 'We better have 5,000 people in the store the first day or you guys are toast.'" The ads ran in high-profile, sophisticated media including the *New York Times*. Oberlander's instincts proved correct: A tidal wave of calls overwhelmed the 800-number listed in the ad, and it had to be shut down.

"There's this whole Tarzhay cult—they love the brand and consider it to be their little secret," Oberlander said. "There are a lot of displaced Minneapolis people and Midwesterners in New York City who have an incredible emotional connection to the brand. My feeling is, you have to get the evangelists excited first. Instead of sending out a broad message to everyone, send a targeted message to people who love the brand to the point of ridiculousness. Get them excited and they'll tell ten friends."

That evangelism is one reason that the Target brand has "tipped"—an expression coined by journalist Malcolm Gladwell in *The Tipping Point: How Little Things Can Make a Big Difference* (Little, Brown & Company, 2000). Gladwell argued that ideas and messages are "social epidemics" that spread like out-breaks of infectious disease—and the moment they reach critical mass is the Tipping Point. These epidemics have three essential characteristics: First, they are driven by exceptional individuals or groups—Gladwell calls them "connectors, mavens and sales-men"—who spread the message. Secondly, the subject of the mes-sage must be "sticky"—it has to be presented and packaged in a way that makes it irresistible. And finally, the "conditions and cir-cumstances of the times and places" in which the message is deliv-ered have to be hospitable.[1] Target hit the bull's-eye on all three accounts: The discount chain has its own group of "connectors"—ardent fanatics who connect emotionally with the brand and en-thusiastically spread the word. The store itself is "sticky"—people wander in and find memorable qualities competitors lack. On the last point, Target arrived in the Northeast at a time when the so-cial context was extremely receptive to its message—a particular juncture in fashion history when cheap chic is cool, in demand, and something people actually boast about. The convergence of those trends tipped the brand—explaining why a store that has been basically doing the same thing since 1962 is suddenly the hottest thing in retail.

Moreover, Gladwell wrote, an inspired, visually arresting ad-vertising campaign can help tip a brand. That's certainly been the case with Target. Oberlander suggested Target play down the "ex-pect more, pay less," motto in its ads, and play up the store's style. "For me, that tagline is a strategy, not a creative expression, and once you say it, it sounds very apologetic," he explained. "We said, stop with the apologies, this is about the democratization of style in fashion trends in this country; that you don't have to spend $400 for sweater, you can get beautiful [cookware] and candle-sticks at a store like this, you don't have to go to Tiffany's. The whole presentation was to talk about style: Looks like Barneys, costs like Kmart."

Target followed up the 800-number ads with a series of stylized, quirky "fashion and housewares" spots, highlighting the range of Target's merchandise. "I literally told my guys to go into the store and walk down the aisles with Polaroid cameras, and try to write stories out of given products," Oberlander recalled. "We just tried to connect the dots: How can we take softlines and couple it with hardlines and maximize the exposure? You always see a model in a cashmere sweater holding an appliance; we decided to take two items and multiply the impact." In one print ad, a waif-like blond in Target apparel is crimping her hair with a waffle iron instead of a curling iron. Another featured a model in a svelte black dress wearing a necklace of socket wrenches. In a third, a pale redhead resembling a present-day Queen Elizabeth sports a black sweater with an auto air filter around her neck—imitating the distinct look of an Elizabethan collar. The ads, shot by photographer Matthew Rolston, had an edgy, urban, high-fashion attitude, and created a buzz. "By hiring Matthew Rolston, that immediately thrust the Target brand into land of Barneys and other retailers," Oberlander said. "So you'd look at the ad and think, oh it's Barneys; wait, the little type says the sweater is $17.99?"

Perhaps the most ingenious aspect of the campaign was that the successful grand opening of the first store wasn't even in New York City. It was in Menlo Park, New Jersey, a suburb about 30 miles south of Manhattan (where the last cutting-edge premiere dates back to 1878 and a laboratory where Thomas Edison invented the light bulb). "We asked Target to take a leap of faith," Oberlander recalled. "New Jersey is too far from New York physically and emotionally; New Yorkers would never say, 'Hey there's a new hot store we need to see in New Jersey.' We wanted to position the grand opening to be the 'New York *area* grand opening.'"

A WINNING IMAGE

Target, which works with an arsenal of advertising agencies rather than retaining one agency of record, took its branding campaign a step further in 1999. Marketing guru John Pellegrene asked Dave Peterson, creative director and founder of Minneapolis boutique Peterson Milla Hooks, to develop a campaign defining Target's spirit. Peterson homed in on the bull's-eye. "It was fun, designery and fashioney," he told Advertising Age, evocative of a Gucci or Chanel logo.[2] The result was "Bull's-Eye World," a retro splash of campy images—blondes dancing around in bull's-eye attire, serving red bull's-eye Jell-O to the tune "Sign of the Times" by Petula Clark (a song Pellegrene had used in a BF Goodrich commercial in the 1960s.[3]) The campaign helped make Target's logo as recognizable as the Nike swoosh. Peterson Milla Hooks followed up with "Pop Art," which included a TV spot featuring a teenager in utility cargo pants gyrating before an array of a psychedelic Tide boxes, while the Canned Heat song "Let's Work Together" plays in the background. Manufacturers clamored to jump on the bandwagon, co-op dollars in hand. "It was the first time I've ever run an advertising campaign where I've had a waiting list in that [Proctor & Gamble Co.] and Pepsico want to be part of it. We're very careful; we actually turned down money and vendors," Pellegrene told a reporter at the time.[4]

In Spring 2001, "Pop Art" evolved into the "Color Your World," campaign, a monochromatic mix of style and substance. One print ad shows three austere models in trendy red Mossimo designs, all angular faces and ebony hair, juxtaposed against scarlet Coca-Cola cans, Pringles cans and Iams pet food bags (being ogled by a red Irish setter). Only the bull's-eye logo—not the store name—adorns the ad. "This is the ultimate emotional connection—when your message is so powerful and so unique that visual expressions can stand alone," said branding expert Marc Gobé of Desgrippes Gobé Group. Advertising Age named Target "Marketer of the Year" in 2000; the next year it won the $100,000 grand prize in the ATHENA Awards for outstanding creativity in newspaper advertising, presented by the Newspaper Association of America. Target also garnered Kelly Awards for 2000 and 2001 from the Magazine Publishers of America, and won the 2001 Heineman Trophy for Best of Show at the 49th annual Retail Advertising Conference.

Experts say Target's campaigns are doing more than winning accolades; they are driving buyers into the stores. "Target's advertising is skewed younger than their shopper base, which is a good strategy if you want to capture consumers before they get too old and have loyalties to other stores," explained C. Britt Beemer, chairman of America's Research Group, a retail consultant, Charleston, South Carolina. "Clearly they are going out to the Gap customers and getting those customers." Beemer's surveys show between 2001 and 2002, Gap/Old Navy lost 22 to 24 percent of their shopper base, and a third of those who left went to Target. "Target is the single biggest beneficiary of that Gap shopper. They are attracting the on-trend shopper," Beemer said. In fact, Pellegrene has cited the Gap, along with Swedish furniture retailer Ikea, as brands he admires. "I think they are the kinds of brands that cross class and income lines," he said in an interview with *Brandweek*. "They have niches that defy the normal definition of a brand—they go up and down. They attract the type of person who drives a Rolls-Royce and those who drive Fords"[5]— Target's aspirations in a nutshell.

The retailer's advertising budget totaled $942 million in 2001, and it continues to spend a disproportionate part of it in New York; splashing the red bull's-eye on billboards, the sides of buildings, and the back of city buses. In November 2002, Target docked a 220-foot-long boat on the Hudson River and offered an array of holiday wares to eager shoppers including an eight-piece martini set and Michael Graves waffle iron. The vessel accommodated 150 people at a time, while waiting guests sipped hot chocolate in heated tents. Transplanted Midwesterner Sabrina Korber, an internet producer, attended the second day of the event. "It was really small but it was a neat idea. The people were so nice. They [Target] had 92 of their top gifts. It was very limited. The products were enclosed in glass so you couldn't touch them. It wasn't the same [as shopping the store] because I like to be able to walk through the aisles and look for bargains. I expected more." In summer 2002, Target wowed jaded commuters with an animated laser-light show inside a subway tunnel in Manhattan. The campaign, created by the agency Submedia, employed hundreds of lights mounted on the tunnel walls. The idea was similar to a child's flip book; the images of models prancing about in bull's-eye logo apparel jumped to life when the train zoomed by them at 30 miles per hour.[6] "New York is the media capital of the world, so it's very important for us to have prime exposure in Manhattan," CEO Bob Ulrich said in a *Fortune* magazine interview. "There's a whole buzz that goes with being seen there."[7]

UNCONVENTIONAL APPROACH

But Target's advertising and promotions department is responsible for much more than creating a buzz around the store and its products. In many retailers, merchants are given the lead on product decisions, while marketers are brought in at the tail end to support sales. At Target, it's the opposite: "We don't look at advertising as purely paper and film," Pellegrene said in a published interview. "We are a dimensional advertising department. We are not a department that simply deals in conventional media. We deal in marketing programs that will also bring millions of dollars into the company in perpetuity."[8]

One such program: Club Wedd, Target's bridal registry, which Pellegrene is credited with inventing. Critics argued no one would register for wedding gifts at a discount store. But the success of the program is one indication that many people no longer think of Target as a discount store: the retailer claims Club Wedd is now one of the largest registries in the world. Target followed up with a baby registry called The Lullaby Club. In addition, Pellegrene has been credited with creating Target's hugely successful "Take Charge of Education" program, through which credit card holders can designate a school of their choice to receive a donation of 1 percent of their Target charge card purchases, and 0.5 percent of purchases made elsewhere on the Target Visa. (See Chapters 5 and 10.) Those using the school program spend four times as much as regular Target customers, according to *Advertising Age*.[9] As of mid-2002, Target had donated more than $67 million to schools across the country. (In the company's September/October 2002 newsletter, it noted that the number one recipient of grant dollars related to charge cards was Columbine High School in Colorado, scene of the worst school shooting in U.S. history in April 1999.)[10]

THE RIGHT CONNECTIONS

While Target's advertising folks come up with novel ways to connect with the customer, they also foster snob appeal—seeking endorsements from the mavens and connectors Gladwell described, by attaching the store's name to the fashion industry's highest-profile events. Every February, for instance, editors, buyers, and paparazzi gather for the hyperbolic convocation of the fashion priesthood known as "Seventh on Sixth"—the fall shows by the designers of Seventh Avenue, held under huge white tents in Manhattan's Bryant Park. In February 2002, the pressroom was sponsored by Target. "They're fantastic," said Peter Arnold, executive director of the Council of Fashion Designers of America, which originally launched the Bryant Park shows in 1993 to showcase American fashion in one venue. Arnold added, "Target has really mapped it all out in terms of where they need to be" among the most influential events and people in style. At an event where the major sponsors include Mercedes-Benz, Piper-Heidsieck champage, Evian, and the ultra-hip W hotels (home of strapping young valets in tight black T-shirts), it is impossible to imagine the elite editors of *Vogue*, *Harper's Bazaar*, or *Elle* rubbing shoulders in "the Wal-Mart pressroom."

"They're brilliant marketers," Oberlander said. "They couldn't have sponsored [Seventh on Sixth] five years ago. If they did, it would have felt just like Wal-Mart doing it. They had to change who they were in the minds of consumers, and what they stood for." Target has also aligned itself with celebrity charities, from the Artists and Writers Softball Game in East Hampton, New York to Broadway Cares: Equity Fights AIDS in Times Square, an annual fundraiser that includes free performances from the major shows on Broadway.[11] Target has also garnered favorable editorial coverage in magazines through its exclusive promotional events. In August 2001, the company decorated a 6,000-square-foot townhouse in Manhattan's Tribeca neighborhood, to preview its home, fashion, and beauty lines for the press, and offered a virtual tour of the house online.

MAUDE FRICKERTT

The emphasis on advertising and promotion is hardly new at Target, but has evolved significantly over the years. The store opened an in-house agency in the late 1960s and produced its first television spots in 1969, hiring celebrity spokesman Jonathan Winters in drag. At the time the comedian was known for his Maude Frickertt persona—a crotchety old lady with glasses and a bun clutching a pair of knitting needles. Winters appeared in commercials promoting store openings in Oklahoma.[12] As early as 1973, Target was refining its newspaper ads with cleaner type and more white space, focusing on a single category of products or one merchandising idea.[13] It launched its Sunday circular, now a must-have among Tarzhay fanatics, in 1975. And Target remains careful not to stray too far from the "pay less" part of its mantra: The Sunday promo continues to emphasize price as well as style. In 2001, items costing less than $10 represented 54 percent of all products promoted in print ads, according to Market Advantage, a Chicago-based research firm, compared with 56 percent the year before.[14]

Target has come a long way since its "Maude Frickertt" days. It continues to forge ties with celebrities, including singers like Tina Turner; and it has been unusually shrewd in backing television programs. "We try to sponsor the hottest things out there in the media we can sponsor," Pellegrene said in an interview in 2000. "Sometimes it's luck."[15] Case in point: Target had the foresight to agree to sponsor "Survivor" in its first season on CBS, a summer ratings blockbuster.

Sports sponsorships remain a long-standing tradition. In 1990, Target became the first retailer to put its name on a stadium—the Timberwolves arena in Minneapolis. The deal was reportedly the brainchild of CEO Bob Ulrich himself; sources told the *Minneapolis Star Tribune* that Target paid just $250,000 for the sponsorship—compared with millions for companies that followed in the retailer's footsteps years later.[16] Target has forged ties with a variety of athletes over the years, from Magic Johnson to Tiger Woods. In fact, Target is a co-sponsor of Woods' "Start Something" program, designed to help young people ages 8 to 17 "identify and achieve their dreams and goals," according to the company's website. Participants work through a series of ten sessions online that help them focus on their goals and develop an "Action Project," through which they learn to take initiative, lead and take care of their communities. Once the program is complete, participants can apply for a "Start Something" scholarship ranging from $100 to $5,000, which can go toward lessons, special educational programs, travel, and equipment. The program gives away $300,000 a year.[17]

For all its associations with the right personalities and the images, the stores themselves are one of the company's best branding strategies, said *Brandweek* senior editor Becky Ebenkamp. She first encountered the discounter in the mid-1980s in southern California, where Kmart was already operating. "[Kmart] was dirty, the cafeteria was disgusting. Target was the same type of store as Kmart, just well-maintained, a really pretty environment with the red color scheme," she recalled. "Over the years, the general impression I got is that Kmart needed to offer something unique to give you a reason to go into the store—first it was Martha Stewart, then Joe Boxer. But Target never had a negative image, they didn't have to worry about upgrading. They're very middle America, but packed with relatively hip things. I think they've done a really good job at making mass a cool place to shop."

⊙ CHECK OUT

Advertising and Promotion

Target's ads focused on evangelists first: They got consumers who were already fans of the brand to spread the word—giving the store more credibility as it moved into the Northeast.

Target emphasizes style in clever and whimsical ways: They use high-fashion images and talent to execute the campaigns; for example, hiring a photographer well known for his work in fashion.

They make smart use of the store logo: A visually potent icon has become interchangeable with the brand itself.

The mission is broadly defined: Rather than simply create ads to facilitate sales, Target's marketing department creates programs that are substantial money-makers for the company, such as registries.

They integrate marketing and philanthropy in ingenious ways: Target's program allows charge card customers to donate a percentage of purchases to support the school of their choice. As a result, those shoppers tend to spend more than others.

They foster snob appeal: They sponsor key events in fashion and celebrity charities.

They make insightful bets on traditional sponsorships: They put promotional dollars behind the series "Survivor" in its first season; they were the first retailer to sponsor a professional sports arena.

CHAPTER 5

Service and Technology

So when you go into Target you think,
yeah, maybe this is the perfect world.
It's like the sun shines. Things are
orderly, they're where they're supposed
to be, people want to help you, they're
friendly to you.

—Howard Ben Tré, Sculptor, Target fan

"A SLEEKER EXPERIENCE"

When Avi and Stephanie Dines bought a home in Framingham, Massachusetts, they did most of their shopping at a Target store a few miles down the road. "My wife is there so often it would be a smart investment for them to build a monorail from our house," he joked. He admits he's impressed too, by the variety of items he can buy in one trip, the ability to shop at unusual hours and the service on the sales floor. When a Wal-Mart opened down the road, Dines decided to check it out. He asked a sales assistant for help. The clerk didn't speak English, so he brought over another worker to assist. That clerk didn't speak English either. "Framingham is a pretty ethnic area, Brazilian and Portuguese," Dines explained. "I understand you have to cater to the communities you are in. But you either need someone who is bilingual, or at the drop of a hat you need to be able to get the information you need from someone else. I'm not thrilled to go back there."

Dines called his Target outings "a sleeker shopping experience" than Wal-Mart, citing a better layout and more upscale feel. "If I need a battery tester, I want to ask someone where I can grab that, go get it and leave," he said. "A lot of times in stores you're waiting and waiting and wondering if you're transparent. At Target, I just think the help is very obvious and blatant; they're roaming around and consistently available, and that makes a big difference."

Rhode Island-based sculptor Howard Ben Tré has had similar frustrations with service. "I remember about 15 years ago we went through this whole thing about how [the U.S.] doesn't make anything anymore, we're a service economy. But there is no service in this country," he complained. "I just stayed at a Westin in Detroit where I had an exhibition open, and Westin is a pretty good chain of hotels. Forget about it—they didn't pick up my laundry when I called them, the service was awful. Coming back, Northwest Airlines lost my bag. When I started complaining to the [service representative], instead of saying, 'Yes, I can understand you're upset,' she said, 'You know, this isn't the most important thing in the world.' I'm like, wait a minute, I have to go home and I don't have any clothes."

Ben Tré's adventures in shopping have been disappointing as well, which was why he was so surprised by his experience at Target. "I was doing an installation in San Francisco, and I needed some little parts of plastic—not something you would necessarily find [easily]," he said. "I went to Home Depot and I went to Staples. In neither store did anyone speak English. I went into Target. As soon as I walked into the store, someone approached me and said, 'Can I help you?' I started explaining, he started to point, and then he said, 'Well actually, let me show you where it is.' Then when I went to check out, there was someone standing there, waiting to tell me which was the shortest line. So when you go into Target you think, 'Yeah, maybe this is the perfect world. It's like the sun shines. Things are orderly, they're where they're supposed to be, people want to help you, they're friendly to you.' "

THE MICKEY MOUSE CLUB

Target didn't always get such high marks for its customer service. In fact, in the 1980s, surveys showed customers wanted more, better, and faster assistance. "We made the decision . . . that we can keep on like we are, disappointing customers, getting low marks on these areas of customer service, or we can bite the bullet and invest the dollars," said George Jones, former executive vice president for store operations, in a 1990 interview.[1] After months of studying various corporate cultures, Target executive Larry Gilpin decided to adopt Walt Disney Corporation's training and service initiatives, and came up with the idea of calling customers "guests" and workers "team members." "He strongly believed in Disney's concepts and Disney's training program," said former Target chairman and CEO Floyd Hall, who was Gilpin's boss in the 1980s. "All good ideas are meant to be stolen, and Disney was considered then—and now—one of the best at customer service."

Target changed its mission statement, declaring it would now be an "assisted self-service" company instead of strictly self-service. In 1989, the company created "Target University" to train workers in its new initiatives, which involved coursework in company traditions, projecting an enthusiastic attitude, understanding customer motivation, and "schmoozing."[2] Target began relaxing some of the rigid rules that made it difficult to address customer needs. It put more workers on the floor to directly assist shoppers, and empowered staff to make common sense decisions, such as offering instant rainchecks and product substitutions. Also, Target decided traditional store visits by company execs had become stiff affairs that intimidated employees and stifled feedback, so visits began to occur more informally, with little advance notice.

Furthermore, Target changed its recruiting, training, and retention programs to better educate staff about its heritage, and to reduce turnover, which in 1989 was 100 percent. "There's a direct correlation between how we treat our employees and how they treat our customers," Jones told a reporter. "It's not realistic to think our employees will treat our customers any better than we treat our employees."[3] Target focused on several initiatives to reduce turnover, including flexible staffing, menu benefits, more support for working parents, and efforts to balance company and employee needs in scheduling work shifts.

A 1991 *Harvard Business Review* study examined service-driven companies, finding that Target (Dayton Hudson Corporation at the time) and several other firms "consciously set out to develop human resources policies and practices that will make them employers of choice, not just in their industries but in the labor market overall."[4] Unlike other retailers, the study said, Dayton Hudson did analyses to determine the characteristics that entry-level employees need to be successful. It also figured out which of those traits were innate, and which could be learned through training. The retailer "prefers to interview ten candidates to find the right person for a job, rather than hire the first warm body who comes along—and then have to fill the same job ten times over," the study noted, adding that Dayton Hudson interviewers favored applicants who saw retail sales as a career.

Former Dayton Hudson chairman and CEO Kenneth Macke first mentioned the new Disney-inspired service changes in 1990, when describing the new Target Greatland retail format to a reporter. He noted the new stores would be 50 percent larger than standard Targets, and boast "a new form of customer service. . . . We're calling it fast, fun and friendly."[5] It doesn't mean customers get the one-on-one attention of a Nordstrom client, but that's not what most Target shoppers are looking for. Customers interviewed for this book consistently said they wanted convenience and accessibility—staff who keep the selling floors clean, the shelves stocked, the products marked with prices—and who are readily available to answer questions without hovering.

"Customer service is extremely important to me because I was previously working for a company involved in customer relations," said Target customer Bob Dzienis. "The more I interact with people, whether it be at an airline or retail establishment, the more frustrated I seem to get. [When] I go to Kmart, it's havoc—clothes on the floor and junk strewn all over the place and no one taking care of it. And on top of that, having to ask someone a question, and they give you that look. I call it the Scooby-Doo look, because they're kind of like, 'Oooor?' That just frustrates the crap out of me. These [Target] people seem knowledgeable of products, or if not, they'll go find somebody who is. They have a more positive attitude in interactions I've seen with customers."

Target closely monitors staff to make sure they deliver on the promise of "fast, fun and friendly." Target store managers reportedly rate workers using a color-coded system: green is positive, yellow is alarming and red signifies a problem. When too many employees fall into the red zone, a district manager appears to deal with the issue and checks in frequently until the situation turns around. The retailer interviews guests twice a year about their treatment in the stores. Meanwhile, each unit reports to headquarters every day on issues like response time to service phone inquiries, checkout efficiency, and returns.[6]

THE WEAKEST LINK: RETURNS

If there is a thorn in Target's garden of customer service initiatives, it is the return policy. The company tightened rules in recent years, and will no longer take back merchandise without a receipt—even from gift registry customers. Angry consumers have aired their grievances on Internet sites like epinions.com and targetsucks.com. The typical protest involves a gift registrant trying to return a duplicate item or exchange something without a receipt—even when the customer wants to spend more for a better model. Target argues its stance on returns matches competitors, and that it had to change the return policy to discourage theft.

But retail consultant C. Britt Beemer calls Target's policy tougher than rivals, and "a major opportunity for disaster. It's an anti-customer strategy. It's come up in our surveys that some consumers look at Target as a discount department store, and they feel returns are part of the way a department store operates," said Beemer, founder of America's Research Group, Charleston, South Carolina. "So they get really irate when they find they have to jump through all these hoops, and many customers are reducing shopping at Target because of it. Target walks a very fine line between irritating customers a little bit and alienating them." Beemer also points out that the more Target builds its gift registries, the more snafus its stringent return policy will create, particularly if gift-givers don't like the practice. "Ultimately they will infuriate their very best customers," he argued. "They make a big deal about giving gift receipts, but I have a hard time putting a gift receipt in a box [with a wedding present]. It doesn't have price on it, but it's something I think is awfully tacky."

Customers who hang on to receipts, though, say they've had smooth sailing through returns. Chicagoan Patti O'Donnell regularly finds herself at Target's customer service counter, because she's often in a hurry and buys clothes without trying them on. "My husband likes to say I don't shop, I return things," she joked. "I buy lots of stuff, and never go in dressing rooms. I also buy baby gifts there. If it's a group buying a baby gift together, I buy a couple of things and let the group pick, and return the other [items]. I never get a question about it."

MANAGING THE PIPELINE

Target's return policy is part of a broader effort to control inventory. In recent years, the retailer has spent hundreds of millions on technology systems and facilities to shorten inventory lead times, deliver more consistent in-stock levels, and reduce markdowns.

For example, store personnel use hand-held scanners that determine how much product is needed on the shelf, weigh that against product needs for the store, and notify the distribution center when the store will need another shipment.[7] Customers have noticed. "If there's something you're looking for and there's only one on the shelf, someone can come over immediately and scan it, and tell you instantly whether there is any more of that item in that store," said New Yorker Tory Johnson. "I appreciate that I can get that information quickly—it shows respect for my time and their time."

Target considers supply chain management to be a crucial component of customer service. In 2001, the retailer opened its first import warehouse to improve processing seasonal and imported goods, and plans two additional facilities in 2003. The company also accelerated expansion of its regional distribution centers— with a goal of doubling the number of facilities between 2001 and 2005. During 2001, in fact, Target achieved the highest levels of in-stocks in its history, according to the annual report. Analysts say Target has made strong progress, but remains a step behind Wal-Mart in technologies that allow retailers and vendors to do joint planning, share data, and improve supply chain intelligence. Target "has the technology to know if they need more smalls or mediums," said Deborah Weinswig, retail analyst, Salomon Smith Barney. "The one thing they don't have is an [online] system called 'Retail Link' that Wal-Mart created. It allows manufacturers to peer into stores and see how their product is selling." But Target has been moving in that direction. In 1999, for example, the company set out to improve communication with vendors by launching a new extranet called "Partners Online," an enhancement to its electronic data interchange. Target and its suppliers can access a database of weekly sales and inventory figures; accounts payable balances; invoice and check information; vendor evaluations; and reference materials, including Target Corporation's vendor partnership manual.[8]

Managing the inventory pipeline is frequently the Achilles' heel of national retailers, noted Cynthia Cohen, founder of Strategic Mindshare, a California retail consulting firm. "You have to consider the whole supply chain, all the way from the merchandise planning function—how many units do I need, at what time—to working with vendors on shipping dates, managing flow through the chain, through the warehouse, to get the right goods to the right stores in the right quantity at the right time. And then doing it all along the way in the most cost-effective way," she explained. "It's a battle every day to keep the lid on expenses, because these are the areas where expenses continually go up—transportation costs, labor. So you can never give up."

Retailers have been racing to adopt proprietary systems like Retail Link to provide a competitive advantage, and many have joined competing Internet-based, business-to-business exchanges. (Target is a member of the Worldwide Retail Exchange, along with 60 other large firms.) Meanwhile the industry as a whole would likely benefit from more standardization, so vendors don't have to adopt different protocols to communicate electronically with their business partners. Target vice chairman Gerald Storch voiced his frustration with inefficiencies in supply chain collaboration in a blunt keynote address at the Retail Systems 2001 and VICS Collaborative Commerce conferences in Chicago. "I strongly believe these exchanges have to come together," he said. "I don't know or even care very much whether it's an official merger or if they all go out of business and start over again. But somehow it has to happen, the sooner the better, because people are on parallel paths spending a lot of money building functionality that doesn't talk to each other. It doesn't make economic sense at that scale."[9]

REAL-TIME CUSTOMER RELATIONSHIP MANAGEMENT

Wal-Mart's systems concentrate on squeezing every last penny out of the distribution structure, so the company can maintain its competitive "everyday low price" proposition. Target's recent technology investments are heavily focused on the customer experience—not surprising given its department store heritage. In 2001, for example, Target became one of the first retailers to roll out a real-time customer relationship management (CRM) system. "CRM is looking through all the data you have on a customer—call center, credit card, people contacting you over Internet—and putting it all in one place, and then searching through the data to figure out who your best customers are, and what kind of products you should be promoting to which customers," explained Barton Weitz, executive director of The David F. Miller Center for Retailing Education and Research at the University of Florida in Gainesville, Florida. "In the broader sense, it's figuring out who your best customers are and getting more share of their wallet." At the bare minimum, CRM helps retailers avoid annoying loyal customers with promotions urging them try a product they already buy. At best, the system allows the store to proactively cross-sell product in other categories, offering shoppers merchandise that complements something already purchased—so a fan of Michael Graves' small appliances might receive information about a new line of kitchen utensils. CRM also facilitates approaching clients through other retail channels, for instance, sending a store shopper a targeted catalog or Web promotion.

The Target system gives the company real-time access to customer data—so if someone orders something on the Internet and calls a customer service center minutes later, the staff can pull up information about the transaction immediately (as well as the client's recent in-store or catalog buys). In 2001, the database contained more than 50 million unique customer profiles.[10] While air-lines and financial services firms have focused heavily on real-time CRM systems, Target is one of the first retailers to do so.

TARGET.COM

Another technological component of Target's service strategy is its website, which has morphed through several incarnations since the late 1990s. When the rest of the retailing world was losing its head in the intoxicating hype of cyberspace, Target took its usual circumspect, Midwestern approach, and in the process avoided some of its rivals' most expensive mistakes. While Wal-Mart and Kmart were collecting scornful reviews for their clumsy websites, and losing money shipping $2.99 bottles of shampoo, Target hadn't even gone online. In 1998, the company bought the Rivertown Trading catalog firm to beef up its fulfillment expertise. When it finally launched a site, the retailer stubbornly adhered to its vision of the Web as a tool for customer service and brand awareness, rather than a sales engine.

"In the early days of the Internet, people got all confused and thought it was all about selling goods online, when it was really about deepening the relationship with the customer," Target Vice Chairman Gerald L. Storch told the *New York Times.* "But I like to say that the stupid era of the Internet is over now." Storch estimated that 100 million visitors visited Target's website in 2001, three to four times the levels of the previous year. "What would you pay for that in TV exposure?"[11] By contrast, Kmart's site, Bluelight.com, opened in 1999; venture fund Softbank invested $62.5 million. Two years later, Kmart repurchased the operation for $15 million and took a $97 million charge against earnings.[12]

In early 2000, Target merged its online operations and direct merchandising to form target.direct, a bit of a mishmash that included multiple websites for its own divisions and operations inherited from Rivertown, as well as old fashion retail catalogs. In September 2001, well after the dot-com meltdown, Target decided to partner with Amazon.com and sell goods on Amazon's site—a fee-for-services deal similar to the arrangement Amazon had with Toys R Us. The executives of both companies first met in January 2000, but made little progress. "Back then, there was too much of a gulf between where we were heading and where they were heading," Storch told the *Los Angeles Times*. "It was like meeting someone from a foreign country, and not being able to speak the same language." Two months later they found common ground, and the two sites started with links to each other. By fall 2002, Target turned over Web operations to Amazon. "Their technology is simply better than anything out there," Storch said. "Everything they do could be replicated [by Target], but it would take years. So why not do it faster?" Analysts describe the deal as a boon to Amazon and an endorsement of its long-term viability.[13]

"I think [the Amazon deal] gives them an edge," said Cynthia Cohen of Strategic Mindshare. "This is a make or buy decision. You can create your own infrastructure for e-commerce, hire people, teach them—but that is expensive and time-consuming, versus going to somebody whose core competency is e-commerce. Amazon already has this knowledge—so [Target is] buying the knowledge—their dollars versus their time frame, their risk. This isn't entirely risk-free, but Target is reducing risk by using knowledge from a company whose core competency is e-commerce."

Online sales tripled in 2001, and traffic to the site quadrupled, according to Cathy David, general manager of Target.com and Marshallfields.com. By fall 2002, Target reorganized its target.direct division to concentrate exclusively on its own brands: Target,

Marshall Field's, and Mervyn's.[14] All of the websites are accessible through Target.com, and the new site also cross-promotes the retail channels: a product search on Target.com yields selections from Mervyn's and Marshall Field's as well. (Target closed a number of Rivertown's catalogs and folded the rest into its website; the upscale "Signals" catalog, for instance, is buried as a boutique within Marshall Field's offerings.)

Meanwhile, profitability remains a close second to intelligence-gathering as the website's raison d'etre—particularly through the emphasis on gifting and registries. "We don't do a lot of flashy merchandising and high tech wizardry . . . for us, our product mix is so broad that what you need by category doesn't work across the whole site," explained David, who spoke at the 2002 National Retail Federation conference. "So what we've done is pretty elementary. We've actually made the shopping experience a little bit different by each category, so the toy shopping experience takes the best of breed . . . in terms of making recommendation by age or by brand or by child interest. In the gift section, it's more, here's the occasion I'm looking for, here's the person, and we'll showcase some of the best gifts that we believe we have on the site. Our focus is really more working with our guests on a behavior basis, what each guest is doing and how to work with that, as opposed to what products are doing." In moving to Amazon's platform, she added, "The idea is understanding the data and being able to use that—that was a big part of what was important to us in the deal." Storch said he expects online purchases to make up 5 percent of the company's overall sales by 2006.[15]

CARDING CUSTOMERS

Although Target has produced some eye-catching advertising, one of its best holiday promotions of 2002 was unscripted. In

November, the *New York Post* ran a full page photo of New York City Mayor Michael Bloomberg, lugging a George Foreman grill and a cheese grater, with the headline: "Why did the $4 billion dollar man get a Target card? To save an extra $2.99." The story explained that the mayor spent $29.99 at a Target in Queens, and signed up for a Target Visa Smart Card to qualify for 10 percent off his total bill. (Target approved a $5,000 line of credit for the mayor, whose personal fortune is estimated at $4.8 billion.)[16]

Rolled out in September 2001, the Visa Smart Card is one of Target's most significant technology and service ventures. The card, which is accepted anywhere Visa is, marked the first time a U.S. retailer launched its own smart card on a mass scale. The card's microchip, with 64k of memory, stores the customers' shopping history, allowing Target to analyze what other retail outlets the shopper is frequenting, what they buy and how much they spend. Target can then push tailored promotions that reflect a specific consumer's tastes. Smart Card users also receive a free card reader that hooks up to a home computer for more secure online purchases, and for downloading store coupons.

The Visa Smart Card is just the latest variation in the company's long history of using credit to build customer loyalty. In the late 1800s, Marshall Field & Co. began offering credit to its biggest spenders "of good moral standing."[17] The balance was not subject to fees or interest, and was to be paid off in full within a reasonable time frame. In the 1930s, Marshall Field's issued a metal card that was useable at branch locations and allowed certain clients to defer payment, but again, no interest and fees were applied to the balance—so the card was chiefly a convenience for loyal clients, rather than a money-maker. In the late 1950s, Mervyn's became one of the first stores to offer revolving credit, and Dayton Hudson followed. Target stores first accepted its parent company's credit cards, and bank-issued cards, in 1972.

In 1994, the corporation reviewed the performance and profitability of its credit card receivables, hoping to save money by farming it out to third-party managers. But studies showed internal management ran the business as profitably as an outside firm could.[18] The company kept the operation in-house, consolidating the two separate receivables divisions (Dayton Hudson/Marshall Field's and Mervyns). The next year, it launched the Target Guest Card, becoming the first mass merchant to offer proprietary credit. By September 2001, 20 million consumers carried the card. But the Target Visa is a much more ambitious effort, with greater potential to boost profits. In the first three months of operations, two million people signed on for the Visa—mostly converts from the Guest Card—driving receivables to $4.2 billion in 2001, up 31 percent from the year before. The average billed balance on the Visa card is approximately five times the amount on a Guest Card, according to an analysis by Bear Stearns, and Target benefits from the fees paid by other retailers who accept the card.[19] In 2001, credit card income totaled $445 million, accounting for 15 percent of the division's pretax profit, and is expected to rise to 20 percent of total earnings, analysts say.[20]

The Visa offers a rewards plan giving cardholders two points for every dollar spent with Target and one point for every dollar spent elsewhere. Once customers achieve 1,000 points, they get a coupon good for 10 percent off at the chain (the certificate has an expiration date, creating an urgency to use it and driving even more dollars into the retailer). Like the old Target card, the new card also supports the chain's popular school fund-raising program (a half-percent of purchases outside Target go to the school of choice.)[21]

Some investors fret about the risks of the credit card business, recalling the troubles write-offs have caused for retailers like Sears. Target counters that its standards are conservative; only a quarter of customers who have the regular Target Guest Card qualify for the Visa Smart Card. In the third quarter of 2002, Target's credit card losses came in at an annualized rate of 7.3 percent, above the default rate for other card issuers such as Citigroup. But, thus far, write-offs have come in well under the loss reserves the retailer set aside for its credit card division. Moreover, Target marketed the card exclusively through checkout lanes and its customer base—no mass mailings, "which highlights the conservative growth and that management is adhering strictly to the primary role the card is supposed to play—deepening the existing guest relationship," a Bear Stearns report noted.[22] In the next chapter, we'll examine the origins of that guest relationship—the visionaries, and the values, that gave birth to Target.

◉ CHECK OUT

Service and Technology

Superior workers: Taking a cue from Walt Disney, Target trained workers in projecting a "fast, fun and friendly" attitude. It put more staff on the sales floor and empowered them to make common sense decisions. It worked to reduce turnover through flexible staffing, menu benefits, and better work-shift scheduling. It favors applicants who want a career in retailing.

Performance monitoring: Staff get feedback on their skills through a color-coded system, and stores report daily on service phone inquiries, checkout efficiency, and so on. Customers are interviewed twice a year.

Managing the inventory pipeline: Target has spent hundreds of millions of dollars on technology systems and facilities to get the right goods to the right stores, in the right amounts, at the right time.

Identifying its best customers: Target became one of the first retailers to roll out a real-time customer relationship management system to better serve its most loyal clients.

E-commerce: Target's website, operated by Amazon.com, is shopper-friendly. It cross-promotes the corporation's retail channels (including Mervyn's and Marshall Field's) and emphasizes registries and gift suggestions.

Credit cards: Target's Visa marked the first time a U.S. retailer launched its own smart card on a mass scale. The card's microchip allows Target to analyze the shopper's spending patterns so it can custom-tailor promotions.

CHAPTER 6

The Legend of George Draper Dayton

Success in any department of life is
attained only through ceaseless industry
and careful thinking.

—George Draper Dayton[1]

SPEED IS LIFE

Although Target was founded in 1962, it's greatest growth occurred roughly over the last two decades, under the leadership of chairman and CEO Robert Ulrich, a lanky, strong-jawed, 59-year-old Midwesterner. Although he took home more than $5 million in salary and bonus in 2001 (and another $10 million from cashing in options), Ulrich eschews designer suits in favor of sweaters, jeans, cowboy boots, and on occasion, $14.99 Target slacks.[2] Ulrich joined Dayton's in 1967 as a merchandising trainee and moved up to president of Dayton Hudson's department stores before becoming Target stores president in 1984. He was promoted to chairman and CEO of Target in 1987, and chief executive of the entire corporation in 1994. Ulrich is reportedly a fan of horses and race cars who likes to kick back with a beer straight from the can and the occasional cigar. The CEO is also known for his generous but quiet philanthropy, particularly to the arts. A divorced father with two children, Curt and Jacqueline, he is protective of his privacy, preferring to put his company in the spotlight. He is also said to dislike public speaking—ironic, in that his bachelor's degree is in journalism and speech from the University of Minnesota. "I'd really rather be in a store with my khaki pants and red polo shirt, and a nametag that just says 'Bob,'" he told a reporter in 1998.[3] In company conference calls, Ulrich is content to handle the formalities and let his right hand men tangle with inquisitive Wall Street analysts. (And Ulrich's inner circle is mostly male—in 2001, 12 of the corporation's 15 executive officers were men, and none of the women worked for the dominant Target stores division.)

But those who know him say Ulrich's low-key, folksy public demeanor belies a razor-sharp strategist who is an intense competitor and demanding boss. Ulrich has no trouble speaking bluntly in private, insiders say; he's reportedly such a straight shooter he earned the nickname "Bullet Bob."[4] In 1994, at his first annual meeting as chairman, Ulrich opened his speech to shareholders and executives with one line: "Speed is life." Lifted from the 1970 Alvin Toffler book "Future Shock"—a tome about the effects of rapid industrial and technological changes—Ulrich made it the corporate motto and had it emblazoned on the company plane. In his first year as CEO, Ulrich eliminated dozens of middle management jobs, seeking to turn the company into a "boundaryless organization"—a notion first espoused by General Electric former chief executive Jack Welch in a 1989 letter to GE shareholders. Ulrich, who admires Welch, sought to break down the barriers and rivalries between the company's operating divisions, to better share ideas and best practices; to take the energy and resources of three separate divisions and unite them into "the power of one," as he has called it. In his first four years as CEO, he would slash $350 million in expenses. (In a speech in Detroit that same year, Welch said: "Boundaryless behavior laughs at little kingdoms called finance, engineering, manufacturing and marketing, sending each other specs and memos and instead gets them all together in the same room to wrestle with issues as a team.")[5]

The "power of one" strategy has had significant implications for the way Target Corporation does business. Buyers from the three divisions share information about hot fashion trends (see Chapter 2), while the discounter's logistical efficiencies are applied to department store operations. "I think he's got good discipline skills. Anyone who works for Bob knows they've got to get the job done," said Floyd Hall, who was chief executive of Target when Ulrich was running the department stores. When Ulrich was rising through the ranks, "everybody had him pegged as a winner, someone who was going to go a long way," said a retired peer. "He was a hard worker and smart, and every job he had, he got good results." His chairmanship has proved no exception: Between 1998 and 2001, earnings rose 21 percent annually, and pretax profit jumped from about $1.6 billion dollars to nearly $3 billion.

Ulrich no doubt has made Target's culture faster, more efficient, and more aggressive—what some call the "Targetization" of Dayton Hudson, culminating in the corporate name change in 2000. But he is essentially applying what he has learned in more than three decades at the corporation. Bob Ulrich was forged in the fires of the Dayton Hudson culture, with a long tradition of hard work, measured risk-taking, disciplined management, and community giving, not to mention a distinctly Minnesotan character—cordial, ethical, unpretentious. One custom particular to the corporate jet, known as "jetiquette," speaks volumes about Target's character. The senior most executive on the plane serves everyone else, taking orders, setting up, handing out the meal trays, and cleaning up. As much as Ulrich admires Jack Welch, it is hard to imagine Welch playing flight attendant, passing out bagels to subordinates. In order to understand Target's unique culture, its leadership, and the strategies that have driven its success, you have go back more than a century and start with the parent company, Dayton's, and the legend of an idealistic businessman named George Draper Dayton. His legacy, and that of his sons and grandsons, remains at the very core of what makes Target tick.

"STERLING INTEGRITY OF CHARACTER"

George Draper Dayton was born in 1857 in western New York, the son of a small town doctor, and descendant of a long line of pioneers. Eight generations earlier, a shoemaker named Ralph Dayton sailed from County Kent, England, to New Haven, Connecticut, later settling in East Hampton, New York. Ralph Dayton helped found the oceanfront enclave in 1649, serving as constable and "interpreter to the Indians."[6] His descendants include Jonathan Dayton, the youngest signer of the U.S. Constitution and the namesake for Dayton, Ohio; and Isaac Dayton, George Draper's grandfather, a schoolteacher who eventually founded Hobart College in Geneva, New York.[7]

George Draper Dayton's parents were deeply religious. His mother Caroline was a member of the Methodist church, his father David, a Presbyterian. Their first home, in Hopewell, New York, was part of the underground railroad, sheltering slaves fleeing the south.[8] George Draper joined the church at a young age and set his heart on becoming a minister, a passion that would inform everything he accomplished later. But he also enjoyed business, and started working at age 11 in a nursery owned by his father for the princely sum of 37½ cents a day.[9] George planned to enter college in the fall of 1873, but larger economic forces would dash his aspirations. After the Civil War, the building of railroads sparked a land speculation frenzy. New York businessman Jay Cooke, whose firm had helped finance the Union army during the Civil War, was building the Northern Pacific railroad, a risky venture that involved 50 million acres of land and sizeable government loans. Cooke's investment firm sold $100 million in bonds to finance the venture, but overextended itself and declared bankruptcy in 1873. Panic ensued on Wall Street. The New York Stock Exchange shut down for 10 days. Banks scrambled to seize assets before they went bankrupt. A financial crisis in Europe prompted lenders to call in their loans from U.S. borrowers. Thousands of businesses failed and millions of jobs disappeared. The panic of 1873 plunged the country into its worst depression ever.

So instead of entering Hobart College, Dayton went to work for George McMillan, a businessman in nearby Eddytown, who had interests in coal, lumber, a nursery, and a vineyard. Dayton's salary was $800 a year plus 3 percent commission, including board. George Draper was such a diligent salesperson that within a year, McMillan owed him $1,500, which he couldn't pay. So he suggested Dayton buy him out. He agreed, and at 17 years old, Dayton was a business owner—and more than $7,000 in debt.[10] Dayton became known for paying his bills early, as well as ardent workaholism: One winter he got the idea of working 24 hours straight, then sleeping a night, and working another 24 hours. Not surprisingly, he ended up quite ill, and his father sold off the business and nursed him back to health throughout the spring. By summer, Dayton was ready to begin again, and signed on with John Mackay, a lumberyard owner, who over the next four years gave Dayton full control of his office and banking business. Mackay later wrote: "I like to think of you, George, and am not a little proud of your manly qualities and sterling integrity of character, and sterling integrity of character is worth a thousandfold more than all the gold of California."[11]

At 21, Dayton married Emma Willard Chadwick, the daughter of a minister, educator, and acquaintance of Ralph Waldo Emerson. (Emma was named for a family friend, educator Emma Willard, who convinced the New York state legislature in 1819 to fund an institution of higher learning for girls—the first state to do so.[12]) Although Dayton earned just $16 a week, the couple set aside $5 a week to invest. By 1883, Dayton's work in John Mackay's business had won him a reputation as conscientious and trustworthy, and he was asked by a group of Eastern investors to look into their mortgage holdings in Minnesota. The state's farmers had suffered through six years of a grasshopper scourge, and a severe winter that caused many to abandon their farms, and their debts.[13] With the help of backers—and having never seen the inside of a bank ledger—24-year-old Dayton purchased the Bank of Worthington, Minnesota, and moved to the upper Midwest, where he began investing in real estate.[14] He straightened out the complex tangle of mortgages that had been sold by a promoter, and found new settlers to cultivate the land. Dayton gave many farmers their start—welcoming those who had little money but good character, providing funds to buy supplies and repair buildings, dispensing agricultural advice, and allowing debtors to pay part of their mortgages in crops rather than cash. (Dayton himself bought 800 acres outside of town with a partner, raising cattle, pigs, wheat and a variety of other produce.) Dayton developed a habit of sending investors their interest checks early, building credibility and positive word of mouth. Along with the bank, he started the Minnesota Loan and Investment Company, which bought and sold real estate. He remained deeply religious, a church elder who occasionally led services at the Presbyterian church, a superintendent of the Sunday school, and a key financial supporter of Macalester College in St. Paul. In a speech at the college some years later, Dayton said: "It sounds somewhat complex, but really it is very simple. Business integrity can be defined to be: Doing things as you agreed to do them. Doing things when you agreed to do them. Doing the things you ought to do."[15]

By 1890, Dayton had outgrown Worthington, and began to study a number of cities for fresh real estate opportunities. He looked at Chicago, Kansas City, Denver, and St. Paul before deciding on nearby Minneapolis, a railroad hub dubbed the "Queen of the Northwest" for its flourishing lumber and flour mills on the Mississippi River. In 1866, The Cadwallader Washburn Mill— precursor of the General Mills Corporation—opened on the river, followed by The Pillsbury Company, which constructed the largest flour mill in the world. Standing on Nicollet Avenue, Dayton evaluated various sites, later recalling: "As I was not known by many in the city, I felt free to stand on corners and count the people pass."[16] He began buying land and buildings in locations others scorned as too far from the downtown, limiting his purchases to

Nicollet Avenue, between Fourth and Tenth Streets—a district that today forms the heart of downtown Minneapolis. "He was very foresighted," said Bruce Dayton, who was close to his grandfather growing up. "He saw in Worthington what the possibilities were before they were developed. He had conquered a rural area, so he wanted an urban area to counterbalance that; and he picked Minneapolis after looking over many cities in the country. That was quite foresighted." Bruce Dayton paused, then laughed, adding: "I always say the important thing is to pick a foresighted grandfather."

George Draper Dayton prospered, but another financial panic ensued in 1893, when President Grover Cleveland called for repealing the law requiring the United States to back its bonds with gold. Imports were halted, European investors fled, credit collapsed, crop prices plummeted and unemployment soared to 20 percent. Railroads demanded payment in advance for transporting sheep, fearing they would not achieve a high enough price upon arrival to cover the freight. Throughout the country, depositors made a run on their banks. Dayton later wrote: "On the morning of July 5, about 10:30 AM, the [Nobles County Bank] closed. . . . As soon as I heard of it, I rushed over and through the back door to ask the president if we could help him. He replied, 'You better look out for yourself.' It had not occurred to me there would be a run on us— we had done nothing wrong. Immediately, however, the run started. . . . It had been the custom of the banks to close from twelve to one o'clock for lunch. I told our people to forget lunch and [stay] open."[17]

Dayton's experience is remarkably similar to the bank run portrayed in "It's a Wonderful Life." In director Frank Capra's 1946 film, banker George Bailey is leaving for his honeymoon when he discovers a run on his savings and loan. He keeps his business open, imploring customers to take only the cash they need and leave the rest—and using his honeymoon stash to keep the institution going. Similarly, Douglas Dayton said when the run occurred on his grandfather's bank, he would "walk around town to get the money back. He ran into one gal with a paper bag and he said, 'What do you have in there?' And she said, 'All the money I had in your bank, George.' And he said, 'Well, I need it worse than you do.'" Like George Bailey, George Dayton used his own money to prop up the bank; he and Emma, now the parents of four children, reverted to the frugal habits of their early married life, even taking in boarders to help pay the bills. At the climax of "It's a Wonderful Life," George Bailey's bank is short $8,000 through an error made by his uncle, and a rival swears out a warrant for his arrest. Friends, relations, and customers come through with the cash—the fruit of years of friendship and good will. During the 1893 panic, Dayton's acquaintances rallied with equal fervor: A former business partner went around town, trading his lumber, machinery, and horses to anyone who had claims against his friend's bank; a man in North Dakota who read about the run in the newspaper wired several thousand dollars, asking, 'Do you need more?' Dayton's old boss, John Mackay, now an elderly man, mortgaged his house and sent the money to Dayton's bank.[18] Such was George Draper Dayton's reputation as a good businessman—and a good man.

The Bank of Worthington survived the financial panic, which endured several years, suffering losses but consistently protecting investors. Dayton ran ads to reassure skeptics: "Interest Always Paid When Due. . . . After a storm, the trees left standing are considered first-class timber."[19] In the meantime, Dayton used what funds he had to acquire depressed stock in other banks—later selling it for three or four times what he paid. In 1898, he sold the bank to focus on his expanding real estate empire. He commuted between Worthington and Minneapolis, finally moving his wife and children—David Draper (known as Draper), Caroline, George Nelson (called Nelson) and Josephine—to a gracious residence on Blaisdell Avenue.

"WE ARE GOING TO MAKE THIS WIN"

Dayton's first project was an eight-story office building on Nicollet and Sixth designed for physicians, dentists, and surgeons. It succeeded despite warnings from local developers that medical people could never comfortably share space in one building. He then purchased the site of the Westminster Presbyterian Church at Nicollet and Seventh, which had burned in an 1895 fire. He contemplated a number of potential development projects for the site before building a retail store. In fact, Target may have never existed were it not for the conservative city ordinances of Minneapolis. Dayton originally negotiated with a group of Chicago developers to build a first-class, 10-story hotel. As the *Minneapolis Journal* explained in February 1901: "Two days ago one of the Chicago men happened to be in Minneapolis with a rough sketch of the plans. He showed this sketch to a Minneapolis friend, and in indicating the fine points of the new building, remarked: 'Here we have a fine bar and billiard rooms.' 'What are you going to sell at the bar?' was the immediate inquiry of the Minneapolis man. 'Soda water and pop are the only liquors you can sell in this town above Sixth Street.' Then he explained the patrol limits system to the Chicagoan, who gasped for breath during the recital. When he recovered sufficiently to enable him to act intelligently, he wired Mr. Dayton and his Chicago partners that the deal was 'dead as a door nail.'"[20]

In 1902, Dayton finally constructed a six-story building at Nicollet Avenue and Seventh Street. "People thought it would fail because it was too far out of town," said Bruce Dayton. "But he was foresighted enough to see that that was the right block, and had the foresight to get one of the biggest department stores in town to move in there as a tenant." To attract customers uptown, Dayton pursued R.S. Goodfellow Company, the fourth-largest department store in Minneapolis, which had been in business for 25 years. The store agreed to move up from Third Street into the expanded space, and quickly doubled sales. Reuben Simon Goodfellow, an Englishman, retired and sold his interest in the store to Dayton, who financed and partnered with a long-time employee, George Loudon, and J.B. Mosher, a retail veteran. Dayton planned to be a silent partner, recalling: "I had no thought or idea of being a merchant."[21]

The opening on June 24, 1902 was heralded by *Minneapolis Journal*: "Thousands of men and women were present at the auspicious formal opening of the new Goodfellow Store. . . . They made purchases, listened to a splendid orchestra and looked with delight at the beautiful goods and beautiful decorations . . . well-dressed and happy-looking clerks were behind the spacious counters ready to answer every query. There are tall glass showcases instead of the old-style shelving and the counter cases are all of glass, fitted with electric lights. On the first floors are to be found silks, velvets, dress goods, trimmings, leather goods, jewelry, perfume, drugs, art goods. . . . On the second floor there are departments devoted to millinery, cloaks, suits, house gowns . . . [and] a number of well-lighted rooms for the fitting of different garments. A splendid display of oriental and domestic rugs and carpets, lace curtains, draperies, blankets, comforters, and artistic furniture is to be seen on the third floor."[22]

Although Dayton was a silent partner, he became more and more involved in the business. At one point he discovered some dishonest financial dealings by one of his associates, and bought

him out for $100,000. A year later, he bought out his other part-
ner. In 1903, he renamed the store Dayton's Dry Goods Company,
and ran the business himself with his son, Draper, who had just
graduated from Princeton. He later wrote: "It was very risky, but
really there was nothing for us to do but go ahead with the store.
We lost money, but we gained experience. I kept track of losses
until they passed one hundred thousand dollars. Then I said, 'I
don't want to know the loss. We are going to make this win,' and
the result speaks for itself."[23] Dayton's gained a reputation for
quality goods at fair prices, catering to a range of income levels,
free delivery by horse and boat, and a liberal return policy unique
for its time. Dayton was also scrupulously honest, offering a dollar reward to anyone finding a mistake in a store advertisement.
The Daytons leased space to other entrepreneurs who provided
services—a beauty parlor, optical shop, a boutique offering hard-
ware, china and glassware, an art gallery, and tearoom. By 1903,
the store turned a profit, and its fortunes swelled with Minneapolis, where the population grew by 100,000 people between 1900
and 1910. Horse-drawn carriages and motorcars crowded Seventh
Street between Nicollet and Hennepin Avenues; the neighborhood
boasted two vaudeville palaces and the luxurious Radisson hotel.
George Draper Dayton had a hand in the latter (perhaps compen-
sating for his unlucky turn with the previous hotel developers):
When a Chicago woman named Edna Dickerson inherited key
parcels of Minneapolis real estate, Dayton and a group of other
merchants convinced her the emergent downtown needed first-
class lodgings. The Radisson opened next door to Dayton's in
1909, where it remains today.[24]

In 1906, George Dayton promoted his 26-year-old son Draper
to general manager. Draper's stated his philosophy this way: "Buy
and sell only merchandise of dependable quality and honest value
at its level. Never buy business through the use of trading stamps

or premiums. Never make unbelievable claims about underselling but never knowingly be undersold. Never claim more than a 50 percent cut in price even if it is true. A claim must not merely be true but credible."[25] In 1909, Dayton's opened its basement store, meant to serve "the very large number of persons in this city who wish to buy dependable, service-giving, and creditable merchandise but cannot afford, or don't want to pay more than is absolutely necessary to secure these qualities."[26] The Daytons also supplied attractions—orchestras, choirs, free lunches, cooking classes—and hatched brilliant marketing stunts. In November 1909, George Dayton cleared the third floor to exhibit the "Curtiss Airship," a bi-plane flown by pilot Glenn Curtiss, who had won a race in Rheims, France. Meanwhile, he negotiated to acquire the real estate around his store. (After his death, Dayton's would expand to 12 stories, running the full block on Nicollet, from Seventh to Eighth Streets.) George Draper and his son also continued to upgrade the interior. In 1910, the *Tribune* wrote: "What management is pleased to term the 'new third floor' is the dream place for women. Nothing could be more elegant or diffuse an air of such utter luxury. Of mahogany woodwork of artistic and costly design, there is no end, and treading the green velvet carpet is like strolling the golf links."[27]

Dayton's younger son, George Nelson, or "G.N.," studied agriculture at Macalester College and the University of Minnesota, and farmed 4,800 acres in Anoka County, breeding Guernsey cattle and Belgian horses. His father and brother convinced him to join the business in 1911, but he kept his hand in agriculture, living from April to October with his wife and five sons on his 800-acre Boulder Bridge Farm on Lake Minnetonka. Draper and G.N. each paid $100,000 for one-third share of the company, eventually buying out their sisters. Bruce Dayton recalled one of his father's executives remarking: " 'For sheer brilliance, give me Draper, but for the long haul, give me G.N.' He was very well organized. All of the strong organization, and I think our people focus came [from him] too."

The Daytons placed a high priority on not only training their people in retail, but also a broader education as well. In 1912, they developed a three-year course of study for employees who had not finished high school. George Draper wrote: "Other stores had plans for teaching the selling of merchandise and the details of completing sales—but we desired something more than that. We wanted to help our youth to equip themselves to become large-minded, intelligent men and women who could grow into better positions and thus become more valuable to themselves, to their employers, and to the world."[28] The school taught arithmetic, composition, salesmanship, dressmaking—but also offered clubs in music, travel, and Shakespeare.

In 1918, George Draper gathered his children and their spouses to witness the creation the Dayton Foundation, "to aid in promoting the welfare of mankind anywhere in the world. . . ." (See Chapter 10.) In subsequent years, George gave so much of his money to the foundation that during the Depression, when his other real estate holdings lost value, he was so short of funds he relied on his store salary to keep him solvent. In time, he became less active in the store and more involved in philanthropy, raising money for a variety of Presbyterian organizations, Macalester College and the YMCA, among other groups. During a 1924 speech at the YMCA, he said: "Character stands out as preeminently the most valuable thing one can seek for, strive for, struggle for in this life. It does not come by chance; it develops slowly and can be easily undermined or wrecked. One must be content to live quietly and gradually prove to the world he is governed by motives that lead him to be honest, truthful, square in his relations to humanity, broad in his friendships, generous in his judgment of others. . . . We sometimes hear people speak laughingly of so-called would-be 'social climbers.' The building of character is a different matter entirely. Character is a matter of slower growth, but the reward is certain. In this world, in the long run, we get just about what is coming to us."[29]

In 1923, Draper was playing golf after work and fell ill. After two days, he died at the age of 43. Sick at heart, his father wanted to sell the store, but Nelson convinced him to stay the course. Two other key managers had died the year before Draper, and the store was in a precarious position. "When he took over the business in '23, Dayton's was a very weak organization," said Bruce Dayton. George Nelson "immediately strengthened the organization, and said he wanted it to be so strong it would never be in that condition again." G.N. hired new managers and refined Dayton's philosophy of service, setting out the following guidelines:

- Capture the customers' imaginations with an array of goods.
- Earn loyalty with a generous merchandising policy.
- Provide incidental attractions and conveniences within Dayton's walls so customers do not wander to the doors of competitors.[30]

Over time, G.N. expanded Dayton's into a 12-story icon that earned a profit every year, even during the Depression—although he continued to honor his father's decision to keep the store closed on Sunday, the Sabbath. Nelson also worked to develop management talent—all male at the time—within the ranks, as he told the *Daytonews*, the company's in-house newsletter: "The only real insurance we can provide is by developing a corps of young men who are potential executives. No amount of preaching is going to develop men to take our places. It is only as we actually put the load on the shoulder of our younger men that we can fit them for the responsibilities."[31] Nelson's sons would later follow this maxim, grooming internal talent and eventually turning the company over to nonfamily management.

In 1928, George Draper and Emma Dayton celebrated their 50th wedding anniversary; she died three years later. "The best recollection I ever have of my grandfather is when my grandmother died," said Bruce Dayton, who was seven years old at the time. "In those days, the coffin was in the living room. She was the first dead person I ever saw, and I was not very comfortable. And he pulled a footstool over for me and I remember the loving look in his eyes when we went to see her to say goodbye; just his gentleness, I'll never forget it."

George Draper Dayton's death in 1937 at the age of 80 was a front-page event in the Minneapolis newspapers. The *Minneapolis Tribune* eulogized his passing: "As a business man, Mr. Dayton was ever faithful to those principles [of Christian living]. The great merchandising enterprise which he founded was solidly foundationed on them, and its sturdy growth reflected, at every turn, the ideals of honesty and service which Mr. Dayton held so dear. In the course of time, that enterprise was to develop into one of the foremost of its kind in the nation and today no little of Minneapolis' reputation as a fine retail merchandising center rests on the institution whose destinies were largely shaped by Mr. Dayton."[32] In short order, the institution shaped by George Draper Dayton would continue its sturdy growth under the guidance of his grandsons, who would retain the ideals of honesty and service as they turned their downtown store into a retailing empire.

◉ CHECK OUT

The Legend of George Draper Dayton

Integrity: Dayton's department store gained a reputation for quality goods at fair prices, a liberal return policy unique for its time, free delivery, and honest advertising. It was also among the early department stores to open a bargain center in the basement to attract lower-income customers. All of the store's strategies were informed by George Draper Dayton's deep religious faith. He defined business integrity as doing the things you ought to do, as you agreed to do them, when you agreed to do them.

Genuine customer care: In his banking and real estate businesses, Dayton invested in people—making loans to farmers with good character but few financial resources. He paid interest to investors early, and earned such a strong reputation for integrity that friends and customers rushed to help when his bank was in crisis.

Bold risk-taking: George Draper Dayton bought his first business at age 17; relocated to the Midwest and purchased a bank without ever having seen a ledger; and took over a retail establishment despite having no experience in the field.

Thinking outside the box: While other developers scoffed, Dayton bought land in Minneapolis based on his own calculations of pedestrian traffic; skeptics who doubted his first venture, a building for medical professionals, were also proven wrong.

Community service: George Draper Dayton started the precursor of the Target Foundation in 1918, provided a $1 million endowment from his personal fortune, and vowed to "aid in promoting the welfare of mankind anywhere in the world."

Emphasis on people: Dayton's started a school for staff who had not finished high school, including basic subjects as well as music and Shakespeare.

Determination: George Draper Dayton successfully conquered two financial depressions, one that thwarted his college aspirations, and another that threatened to take down his bank. When he started in retailing with his son, initial losses soared to $100,000, but he would not give up, turning the loss into a profit the next year.

CHAPTER 7

The Next Generation

You can discount at any quality level.
Partly because of our heritage, we decided
that the soundest position was to establish
ourselves as the quality discounter.

—Douglas Dayton, Target president, 1966

"YOU COULDN'T TAKE ADVANTAGE OF YOUR POSITION"

Just 20 minutes outside Minneapolis, off a two-lane gravel road near the shores of Lake Minnetonka, Bruce Dayton keeps an unusual "home office." It's a *house* office, actually. He works in a charming, sunflower yellow cottage surrounded by tall trees, about a quarter mile from his home. The solid little structure is vintage 1960s inside, yellow-green linoleum and pale maple kitchen cabinets in pristine condition. Narrow stairs lead up to a sunny, loftlike living area with a vaulted ceiling, whitewashed walls, tweedy rust-colored couches, and a triangular glass coffee table. A low bookshelf on one wall holds several volumes on retailing, along with a stack of *Fortune* magazines, some the same vintage as the house. The rooms are adorned with art—modern, Chinese, classical German paintings, bronze horse sculpture; Bruce, a board member of the Minneapolis Institute of Arts, has also collected Matisse and Mondrian. A huge bedroom down the hall is furnished with an enormous mahogany desk, a computer, and a Reuters terminal (Bruce Dayton has followed the stock market since college). In his early eighties, he is casual in a camel-and-black houndstooth blazer, white shirt, tan slacks, and brown hush puppies. He grins as he recalls buying the house in 1973. "One day, Oscar Olsen, a Swede who built a lot of the homes in the area, came up to me and said, 'Dayton! My wife and I are getting too old for this place. We're moving to an apartment. Do you want to buy my house?' I said, 'How much?' He said, '$19,000.' I said okay, and he went, 'Whoopee!' "

Across town in the Interchange Building, a sleek glass office tower near the General Mills headquarters, Bruce's youngest brother, Douglas, works in a slightly more formal setting. It's a modest space, simply furnished with a desk, sofa, and filing cabinets. Two eastern windows showcase a spectacular view of downtown Minneapolis. Paintings of birds adorn the walls, and there are photos scattered about, including a younger Bruce wearing a heavy leather glove with a falcon perched on his arm—a hint of his devotion to conservation causes. In his late seventies, he is dapper in a white tailored shirt, slacks, suspenders, a green tie embroidered with ducks, a seersucker jacket, and brown wingtips.

Their styles and interests may be different, but the Dayton brothers are a tight-knit group. Bruce is now the oldest of the three surviving Dayton brothers; brother Donald died in 1989, and Wallace in 2002. Bruce stays in close touch with Kenneth and Douglas. "We were raised altogether and got along very well together," he said. In 1988, a year before Donald died, he entrusted Bruce with a scrapbook containing material their grandfather had saved from 1869 to 1937. Working with historian Ellen B. Green, Bruce Dayton privately published a 527-page biography of his grandfather in 1997. The summer of our meeting marks the 100th anniversary of the grand department store his grandfather created. But aside from a photo of George Draper in the cozy loft, the only other prominent evidence of the family legacy is a white toy trailer truck on the coffee table, adorned with a red bull's-eye and the word *Target*. "We had a great opportunity handed to us," he said. "We weren't out to prove anything. We just wanted to do a good job."

The Dayton boys grew up in a house on Blaisdell Avenue just down the block from their grandfather George Draper, at whose home they ate many Sunday dinners. From April through October, they lived at Boulder Bridge, their father's 800-acre farm, where they cultivated oats, hay and corn, and raised prize-winning live-stock. "We worked in the mornings for 10 cents an hour, down in the barns, and played in the afternoon," Bruce recalled. Douglas remembers games of cowboys and Indians on horseback, swimming in the lake, and smoking corncob pipes. "I was a driver's helper on the farm truck, mostly what we hauled was manure," he said. "Load by hand, unload by hand. We had a wonderful bunch of farmers to work with and you worked right alongside them. You couldn't take advantage of your position."

The Dayton brothers spent their lives not taking advantage of their positions, which may be part of the reason for Target's enduring success. Although they were sons of the boss, the third-generation owners of Dayton's, they started their careers on the lowest rungs of the retailing ladder. Donald joined the family business in 1937 as a stock boy after graduating from Yale. Bruce and Ken, both Yale graduates as well, took jobs in merchandising. Wallace, who studied at Amherst, started behind the cosmetics counter, and Douglas, who graduated a few years behind his brother with a history degree, sold ladies shoes on the balcony. He displayed an early flair for sales. "I didn't know how to put a shoe on a lady's foot to start with, and it took me a while to figure out how the boxes ran in the stock room," Douglas recounted with a grin. "I'll never forget one shoe, it was a sling pump, patent leather on one side. I thought they looked great so I pitched 'em and sold 'em, and everyone was laughing at me when I came in the back. I said, 'What's the matter?' They said, 'Well, don't you know, there's a $4 spiff on that shoe.' We'd 'spiff' the merchandise— giving the salesmen incentive to sell it, rather than mark it down. Well I didn't know the difference, but they were so tired of that shoe—they thought it was a dog."

The four younger Daytons served in World War II; Donald, whose childhood bout with polio prevented him from enlisting, kept the ship afloat until his brothers returned. In 1947 Donald was named general manager. In 1950, their father, George Nelson Dayton died of cancer, and the sons took full control, each with 20 percent of the business. "I was young at the time," the late Donald Dayton said in a 1979 interview, "and we had a hell of a responsibility just to keep things going."[1] They faced serious challenges: Six of the store's key managers had retired in the late 1940s, and their Minneapolis flagship required renovation. It was a substantial business, the nation's second largest family-owned department store after Hudson's in Detroit, boasting $50 million in annual sales. It had also captured about all the business it could handle. "One store wasn't big enough for five boys, and we had to figure out a growth plan," said Bruce. They spent Saturdays at the Radisson Hotel next door—the place their grandfather had convinced Edna Dickerson to build more than 40 years earlier—hashing out the future of the business. "We soon decided that we were paying too high a price for harmony, and that profit would be our goal, not harmony," he continued. "Because in the long term, profit would produce harmony and lack of profit would produce disharmony. We got along very well. If we had an issue, we took a vote, and three votes won."

The Dayton brothers wanted to do more than keep things going—they were empire builders, who grew up listening to their father's and grandfather's nightly tales from the store. (None of the Dayton boys studied business in college. Douglas Dayton says the only D he received at Amherst was in economics.) "I would describe them as bright, hardworking, driven and really, they drove each other," said Norman McMillan, a Target executive who joined the firm in the late 1960s. "They were very ambitious to be the best—they weren't happy with being second. Here they were very wealthy men, the sons of a very successful father and grandfather, but they were always trying to prove to each other they were as good as those guys. I thought they were quite competitive, very ambitious for the company."

The Daytons started with branch stores, opening a second department store in 1954 in downtown Rochester, Minnesota, two blocks from the Mayo Clinic. Douglas was tapped to lead the operation. Shopping centers followed: In 1956, Dayton's made retailing history, constructing the first enclosed mall in the country. It included Dayton's department store and its largest rival, Donaldson's, along with 75 other shops on two levels. It was developed in a 500-acre cornfield southwest of downtown Minneapolis, where Dayton's affluent customers were buying suburban homes. The brothers also launched a real estate arm—Dayton Development Company—to oversee its properties. In 1959, they purchased Schuneman's department store in downtown St. Paul, expanding the store by 40 percent and adding a parking garage.

With each new venture, they reinforced the retailing principles they had learned from their father and grandfather: quality, value, and service, including home deliveries, sometimes twice a day. They wanted as much market share as possible—from the couture business in the store's Oval Room to the sales of modestly priced wares in the Downstairs Store. "I would say dominance was our objective; we didn't say that, the lawyers didn't like that word," said Bruce Dayton. "But for instance, of the stationery department in front of the store, we would say, 'Now is that the best bridge card section in the Twin Cities? Was it dominant? Was it as good as it could be?'" Douglas Dayton recalled the company's conservative lawyers also banned the use of the word "guarantee," but the notion was implied in everything Dayton's sold. "We used to have a garden store downtown, and one customer asked the manager, 'Can you guarantee that this plant will live?' And he said, 'Ma'am, we can't use the word guarantee, but if I ever saw a plant that has the will to live, this one has it.' "

Dayton's liberal return policy continued to be a winning strategy with customers as well. Douglas Dayton recalled a customer who came in to return a dress that was at least a year old. One of Dayton's "floor walkers," who worked in returns, politely asked why the woman wanted to return the dress, since the store would be unable to resell it. The woman replied, "Well, it doesn't fit anymore," Douglas recalled. The fast-thinking clerk suggested the store tailor it for her. "She was happy, and we didn't have to take back something we couldn't sell that had already been worn." That return policy was crucial; a later survey found that 80 to 90 percent of customers said the number one reason they shopped at Dayton's was because they knew they could get their money back. "There wasn't nearly the problem with returns then that there is now," Douglas Dayton added. "We used to say, 'It's not whether the customer is right; it's whether she *thinks* she's right.' "

Meanwhile, the Dayton brothers added new attractions to the downtown store, including an elaborate annual Christmas display. "The windows on Nicollet Avenue were very well done, and we had an arcade in the toy department with a train and chimpanzees," Douglas Dayton recalled. "One year they had some live reindeer. A kid grabbed the reindeer's horn, and the horn came off." Fortunately, the reindeer was unharmed, and the attraction would blossom into a full holiday village and pageant in the eighth floor auditorium, continuing to attract half a million visitors between Thanksgiving and New Year's today.

The Malling of America

By the early 1950s, both Dayton's and J.L. Hudson's had established themselves as retail innovators—setting new standards for excellence in product quality and service. Both cultures were conservative and hierarchical, but forward-looking. Both companies took their cues from customers, proactively brainstorming about the next wave in the business, supporting ideas with research and when the decision was made, acting boldly, investing confidently and striving to make the venture the best in the business. So in the 1950s, when the two companies decided to cater to their customers on new turf, they achieved design and technological breakthroughs that made history. Just two years apart, relying on the vision of the same architect, the family-owned retailers opened extravagant shopping malls that irrevocably changed Americans' shopping habits and lifestyles.

Shopping centers began springing up in the United States as early as the turn of the century; they generally consisted of a group of stores built and leased by one developer and located at a busy intersection with ample parking. But the Depression and World War II slowed their development, and by 1946, there were still just eight shopping centers in all of the United States.[2] In 1950, Northgate, considered to be the first regional mall, opened on a 50-acre site outside Seattle. It was designed by Jack Graham Jr., who at various times in his career had worked as a retailer, real estate developer, and architect. Northgate differed from earlier shopping centers because Graham purposely anchored each end with a department store, and oriented 40 smaller stores inward along a 40-foot-wide, open-air pedestrian walkway. Graham called it "the mall"—the first recorded use of the word in connection with a shopping center. He was also the first to use marketing studies and traffic analysis to choose the site.[3] Northgate was located next to a highway, as its successors would be, and offered some freestanding businesses, including a gas station, bank, and movie theater. The 4,000-car parking lot occupied 75 percent of the site.[4]

Around the time of Northland's construction, Victor Gruen, an Austrian architect who had escaped the Anschluss more than a decade earlier with eight dollars in his pocket, found himself in Detroit on a small project. He toured Hudson's, the 25-story downtown retail palace that rivaled Macy's in size, but served a metropolis with just a quarter of the population. Like Graham,

Gruen was also an advocate of analysis, and he decided to research growth trends in Detroit. He returned to his office in Los Angeles, took his findings and drafted a ten-page proposal explaining why Hudson's should build a branch store and a shopping center. He sent it to a Hudson's executive (who had never heard of Gruen), and received a letter in response inviting him to drop by the next time he was in Detroit. In the meantime, Hudson's management was doing its own number-crunching. The team included four nephews of founder J.L. Hudson, the Webber brothers—Oscar, Joseph, Richard, and James—as well as James' son, James Jr. They had stubbornly opposed expansion beyond the downtown flagship, but abruptly changed course when the 1950 census figures showed explosive population growth—200 percent plus—on the outskirts of Detroit. Meanwhile, the city's core had grown less than 25 percent.[5] Once convinced, the Webbers moved boldly: planning not one, but three major shopping centers on Detroit's perimeter.

Gruen had never built a shopping center before he convinced Oscar Webber, Hudson's president, to construct the largest one in history—on a 400-acre plot with a $30 million construction budget. At the 1952 groundbreaking, Gruen reportedly turned to his partner, Karl Van Leuven, and said, "My God . . . we've got a lot of nerve."[6] The seeds were now planted for what one editorialist would later christen the "gruening" of America.[7]

Gruen embedded Hudson's in the center of the mall, and configured 80 stores around it in a square—designing wide pedestrian concourses broken up by lavishly landscaped courts and terraces. Among the inspirations for Northland: the medieval market towns of Austria and Switzerland that Gruen had toured on bicycle years before.[8] Hudson's location was designed to enhance the success of the center as a whole: Shoppers had to walk past competing stores before they reached the department store, and only 12 percent of the parking area had direct access to Hudson's. Gruen had studied with modernist Peter Behrens—a mentor to Mies van der Rohe and Le Corbusier—and so his framework and colonnades were composed of strong, minimalist lines; but individual stores were allowed to design their own fronts (with approval), to emulate the colorful variety of a downtown shopping district. In 1954, *Architectural Forum* heralded the center's "uninhibited, generous and lighthearted use of art . . . Northland's sculpture has the verve, the inventiveness and the simple joy in life of fine children's book illustration."[9] Gruen advocated the shopping mall as a civilizing antidote to suburban sprawl and the dominance of the automobile, a place where the community could gather for all kinds of activity: The Northland complex included everything from public meeting rooms to a supermarket. As one astonished visitor would later describe: "In a single visit to Northland, a family can get haircuts and permanents, take out insurance, arrange a world tour, get a medical examination, have dental work done, obtain up-to-the-minute stock quotations, enroll in bridge and sewing classes, have eyes checked, prescriptions filled, clothes dry-cleaned, pictures taken, watches repaired, shoes shined, and even the dog washed."[10]

Reflecting the Webber brothers' old school approach, Northland's public opening was a quiet event—no inaugural celebration, promotions, or even newspaper ads. Hudson's mailed invitations to neighbors and credit card customers, and held a press preview a full week before the launch, to allow some of the fanfare to die down. The only preview the Webbers considered important was the one held for the 12,000 employees of the downtown store.[11] Northland opened in March 1954 and blew away forecasts, taking in $78 million in its first full year—double expectations. Attendance, forecast at 30,000 a day, ran as high as 50,000. Northgate's achievement changed the blueprint for retail success—and department stores began to build malls in droves.

Victor Gruen's next project, in Edina, Minnesota, topped Northland on a number of levels. But its most remarkable accomplishment was the ability to thwart Minnesota's severe weather—which was suitable for outdoor shopping only about a third of the year. Hired by the Dayton family, Gruen took his inspiration from the glass-domed Galleria Vittorio Emanuele II in Milan, and proposed a two-level, roofed complex that would be heated in the winter and air-conditioned in the summer. "Victor Gruen was very nice, a fine architect," Bruce Dayton recalled. "He came up with the idea. He tried to sell it to somebody in Houston, but that fellow backed out and then he brought the plan up here." Southdale, as it became known, was also unusual in its choice of key tenants. In a 1991 interview, Dayton Hudson's head of move planning, Glenn Fuller, recalled: "Southdale had everything. But what really made it special . . . was the leasing. Dayton's went to all the major retailers in the area and recruited only the best for the mall. They even got Donaldson's, their primary competition, to come into the center. This was no mean feat when you consider that these guys really hated each other. From the very beginning, Donald Dayton wanted only the best in that center, even if it meant helping the competition."[12]

Gruen placated the rivals by anchoring one on each end of the mall, installing a huge courtyard between them, and lining 75 stores along the mall on two levels. "We gave them their choice; they went in the southeast corner and we went northwest—there were more people when we opened in the southeast than the northwest," Douglas Dayton explained. The enclosed space sported a three-story, skylit garden, 21-foot cage filled with exotic birds, a fishpond, towering tree-like sculpture, fountains, and a sidewalk café. A children's play center in the basement included a small zoo. Individual shops were able to design storefronts using wood, plaster, and crystal—materials that would have been unfeasible in an outdoor setting. Because the negotiations between Dayton's and Donaldson's dragged on for a year, Gruen's team had time to plan efficiencies into the physical plant: loudspeakers that piped in Muzak during the day could be reversed at night to detect any sound in the stores. An unusual heating/cooling system saved $500,000. At the opening, the Daytons figured they would need attendance of 20,000 a day to turn a profit; on some days Southdale attracted 75,000. The center cleared $30 million in its first full year, although some smaller tenants say it took a few years for their stores to turn a profit. "The center was so family-oriented and such an attraction that people would often gawk instead of shop," one former small-store owner groused.[13]

Gawking was fine with Gruen, who felt he'd created a concept to conquer suburban sprawl. "I remember the surprised faces of some of my clients when we drove out to a shopping center on a Sunday and found the courts and malls, the lanes and promenades, filled with milling crowds dressed in their Sunday best," Gruen later wrote. "They engaged in an activity believed to be long forgotten, that of leisurely promenading while enjoying the flowers and trees, sculptures and murals, fountains and ponds."[14]

The success of Northland and Southdale had launched a wave of covered malls. From 1960 to 1970, more than 8,000 new shopping malls opened in the United States—double the previous decade. Architect Victor Gruen, recognizing what his invention had wrought, bitterly tried to reverse the hands of time: In 1964, he refocused his architectural practice on revitalizing downtowns through the creation of pedestrian malls—to little avail. Defeated, he returned to Vienna three years later, and retired shortly thereafter. (He would later renounce huge suburban regional malls, telling a columnist in 1978, "I refuse to pay alimony for these bastard" products of "fast-buck speculators and promoters.")[15] That same year, Dayton's exited the mall business, selling Southdale (and eight other malls) to the Equitable Life Assurance Society of the United States for $305 million in cash and debt. By that time, Southdale had expanded to one million square feet.

THE DISCOUNT THREAT

While the brothers were successfully expanding their upscale retail business, they were also planning to dive into one of the fastest growing parts of the industry, mass retailing. According to *Discount Store News*, by 1962, the discount industry was a $4.25 billion dollar business with 1,500 stores, led by 14 chains that together had more than $1 billion in sales.[16] That year became a watershed in modern American retailing. S.S. Kresge opened its first Kmart in Garden City, Michigan—the result of a yearlong study of discounters by Harry B. Cunningham, who became CEO. Sam Walton, at age 44 the largest franchisee for Ben Franklin's variety stores, opened his first Wal-Mart Discount City in a 16,000 sq. ft. space in Rogers, Arkansas. And Dayton's launched its first Target in Roseville, Minnesota. "Kmart was founded by a dime-store company, Wal-Mart was a variety store company," explained former Target executive Norman McMillan, founder of the retail consulting firm McMillan/Doolittle, based in Chicago. "The background of the Target enterprise was the department store business—so that influenced our strategic planning and the way the stores were run."

The Dayton brothers' decision was not wholly appreciated by their peers. In a 1966 speech before department store executives at a meeting of the Associated Merchandising Corporation (AMC), Target president Douglas Dayton found himself defending their new enterprise: "I start with the assumption that all of you . . . wish that discount stores had never been invented, and I have no quarrel with that wish. It is a perfectly natural one. The catch is that it doesn't seem to have impaired discount stores' progress one iota. I am going to try to document for you the validity of our performance in order to convince you that discount stores are a vital part of our retail distribution system," Dayton said. "To some I may be laboring the point; to others—and I have to be perfectly frank—you have underestimated what is going on."[17]

In 1914, Lincoln Filene, owner of Filene's of Boston, got the idea to form an association of prominent department stores to share ideas and sales figures. Called the Retail Research Association, it included Dayton's, Bloomingdale's of New York, Abraham & Straus of Brooklyn, Lazarus of Columbus, J.L. Hudson's of Detroit and Strawbridge & Clothier of Philadelphia. In 1918, the group became the Associated Merchandising Corporation, a cooperative buying agency that sourced fabric, goods, and production overseas. AMC had offices in London, Paris, Milan, Vienna, Brussels, and Tokyo. Its meetings provided a place for retailers to hobnob and benchmark performance—a brotherly spirit of collusion where Dayton's women's wear buyers could compare notes with counterparts, since none of the stores had branches competing for the same customers. They shared a common accounting method, and once a year, AMC published a "Red Book" of the best performers by department. As late as the mid-1960s, some members of the clubby AMC still disdained discount stores as the industry's bastard children—or as Douglas Dayton's speech diplomatically noted, "of ignoble birth." Some department stores that offered a discount area seemed to do so grudgingly. As one former Hudson's executive said of the Detroit flagship: "There was a basement store, but it was clearly the basement store—it was today's Wal-Mart. And if you went down in the basement store, you were of a different class."

The First Discounter

In 1885, a brash 27-year-old retail executive named Harry Gordon Selfridge approached his boss, Marshall Field, with a bold idea for the company's flagship Chicago store. For a number of years, Marshall Field & Company had used a portion of its basement to unload off-price goods. Selfridge, a flamboyant showman who would later launch the department store Selfridge's of London, saw an opportunity. He argued that an expanded bargain center could capture customers who would otherwise avoid the marble palace on State Street. "We must give the shopper there the same service and honest representation of goods—and she will come back again and again!" Selfridge said, convincing Field that the bargain shoppers, or their children, might eventually gravitate to the store's upper floors. In its opening week, The Budget Floor attracted thousands of shoppers, who snapped up cheaper silks, embroideries, gloves, cloaks, and shawls. Field's basement mushroomed into the largest single salesroom in the world, grossing $25 million a year.

Source: Adapted from Lloyd Wendt and Herman Kogan, *Give the Lady What She Wants: The Story of Marshall Field and Company,* (Chicago: Marshall Field & Company), 1952, p. 204.

WANTED: BRAND NAMES AT BARGAIN PRICES

After World War II, savvy merchants saw opportunity in a growing group of classy customers who wanted better values. The economy was surging, the baby boom burgeoning and city dwellers scattering to suburban homes sprouting among the fallow potato fields of Long Island and the cornfields of the Midwest. A new prosperity fueled demand for durable goods and designer names—GE appliances, RCA television sets, Parker pens, Zippo lighters. In fashion, women of all incomes aspired to Christian Dior's New Look, with the nipped-waist and dramatic flared skirt—a backlash against the stringent cloth quotas of the war years. Chunky cork or wood-soled "wedgies" gave way to Charles Jourdan's sexy stiletto high heels. The *Saturday Evening Post* teased, "The girl with low and sensible heels is likely to pay for her bed and meals."[18]

But consumers found no matter where they shopped, coveted brand names were usually sold at similar prices—a vestige of a Depression era program called the National Recovery Administration (NRA). Part of the New Deal, NRA devised codes of fair competition to regulate the economy, fixing prices so that producers had to charge every retailer the same amount, no matter how large their orders. If larger stores could get discounts and pass them on to customers, the theory went, smaller mom-and-pops would be forced out of business—eliminating more jobs at a time when the national unemployment rate stood at 25 percent.[19] In 1935, the NRA was declared unconstitutional, but the philosophy of price-fixing continued. In 1937, Congress passed the Miller Tidings amendment to the Sherman Act. It created anti-trust exemptions for certain agreements fixing minimum suggested retail prices for some branded products. Miller Tidings effectively allowed name brand manufacturers to force stores to sell their goods at the suggested retail price, and no lower.[20]

In 1948, a Brooklyn-born entrepreneur named Gene Ferkauf found a loophole in the federal law: He established a "membership store." Ferkauf opened his first E.J. Korvette in a second-floor shop on 46th street near Fifth Avenue in Manhattan. It barely resembled a retail establishment, devoid of any window display or signage. Clerks loitered in front, handing out flyers that contrasted recommended retail prices with Korvette's—which were usually one-third lower. Shoppers were told the stores were for members only and then given free "membership cards." Word of the tiny operation spread quickly, and in the first year, Korvette sold nearly $1 million in goods in cash—a whopping $2,500 a square foot. Between 1950 and 1956, *Fortune* magazine noted, sales skyrocketed more than 2,600 percent.[21]

While Ferkauf was dodging the price police in Manhattan, veteran retailer Martin Chase was shaping an entirely different discount concept in Cumberland, Rhode Island. In 1953, Chase took over a defunct mill called Ann & Hope. Rather than brand names, he began peddling off-price merchandise, starting with a bundle of ribbon from a bankrupt textile company. It swiftly sold out. Ann & Hope established a new prototype for the emergent industry: The store was largely a self-service affair—a concept that began amid the labor shortages of World War II. It provided shopping carts—an innovation of the 1930s and a rarity beyond supermarkets at the time—as well as a huge parking lot. Wal-Mart founder Sam Walton was just one of many retailing executives who made the trip east to check out Ann & Hope and E.J. Korvette.

Chains such as Arlans, J.M. Field, Interstate Stores, Shoppers Fair, and Spartan followed E.J. Korvette and Ann & Hope into the business. "The coming of the discount stores was a huge threat," recalled former Hudson's executive Ed Yager. "We spent a tremendous amount of time as executives touring E.J. Korvette and the other discount stores as they opened, because that model was so completely different from high-service model we were used to. It was a very, very different kind of business model in terms of the customer and the customer contact." As one customer said of her service experience at Korvette: "I know why things cost so much more at Macy's. There they treat you like human beings."[22]

In 1961, the AMC meeting was held at the historic Greenbrier Resort in White Sulphur, West Virginia. Ira Hayes, a representative of the National Cash Register Company, the industry's dominant vendor, delivered a two-morning seminar on the wild success of discount stores. "That's what ticked off our investigation of the business," Douglas Dayton noted. "We looked at several discounters. Topp's in Chicago was the first layout we saw that we liked. In those days, you couldn't write notes or take pictures in a discount store; the manager knew what we were doing. He said, 'I'm sorry you can't write inside.' So we would pace off the departments, go outside and write down the dimensions, and then come back in."

"We figured rather than let [discounters] come in . . . we would start our own," said Bruce Dayton, pointing out that Dayton's already had a thriving, low-priced Downstairs Store that operated separately from its department stores. At one point the Downstairs Store was the fourth largest store in Minneapolis, after Dayton's, Donaldson's, and Sears. But a new discount division would give the brothers the opportunity to expand anywhere they wanted to go. Moreover, the Daytons saw an opportunity to be the diamond in the rough world of mass retailers. As Douglas Dayton explained in his AMC meeting speech, "You can discount at any quality level. Partly because of our heritage, we decided that the soundest position was to establish ourselves as the quality discounter." Douglas, who had once run Dayton's Downstairs Store, was named president.

The man who helped him position Target at the high end of the new discount industry was a merchandising guru and 13-year Dayton's veteran, John Geisse. Geisse saw mass retailers as the perfect complement to department stores—the ideal model to capture the value-oriented "basement" shopper who sought a higher-quality experience. A workaholic father of ten children, Geisse had considered leaving Dayton's to start his own company, but lacked capital. Instead he pushed hard internally for a discount division, and joined the new business to oversee creation of the concept, the store environment, and operations. "For the first several years we had a very effective working relationship. He was a darn good merchant, with a very good sense of detail," Douglas Dayton recalled. Dayton's publicity director Stuart Widdess and his staff debated more than 200 possible names for the new venture before settling on Target. The next step was a designing a proper logo. "I remember going through different versions—we even had one Target with three bullet holes through it, which even in the 1960s we decided wasn't appropriate," said Douglas Dayton, chuckling. "And we had a couple extra rings in it early on. So it's been modified somewhat."

With a $4 million investment from the parent company and a handful of staffers, Target began its rollout in the suburbs of Minneapolis-St. Paul. In the first few years, its managers would make some costly mistakes, but the Dayton brothers were committed to the concept. At the time, they didn't necessarily know that discount stores were the wave of the future, but "we did know department stores were a dying breed of cat," said Bruce Dayton. "Even though they were very successful—big cash generators and still are—they didn't work for the long pull. We had as much share of market as anybody, so there wasn't any growth opportunity in a department store. Whereas Target, you can go anywhere." In the next chapter, we'll look at where they went, and how they would lay a foundation of professional management that would carry Target beyond the brothers' boldest expectations.

⊙ CHECK OUT

The Next Generation

Staying humble: All five Dayton brothers started at the bottom of the ladder, in the stock room or sales floor, so they understood the business from the ground up.

Focusing on profit: The Daytons made a conscious decision to focus on profit rather than group harmony, reckoning that a profitable business would bring harmony, and an unprofitable one, disharmony. Decisions were made through a majority vote.

Starting with the familiar: The brothers first expanded by opening a branch store, building on a business they knew well before moving into new formats.

Thinking and investing boldly: When the Dayton's decided to develop a mall, they made history by creating the first enclosed mall in the country.

Staying true to their values: Each new venture reinforced the principles the Dayton brothers learned from their father and grandfather: quality, value, and service, including a liberal return policy. When they entered the discount arena, they developed a concept that was authentic to their heritage, the "upscale discounter."

CHAPTER 8

Management Excellence

Duluth was the first place I heard it:
Customers started calling it
"Tarzhay." That was 1962.

—Douglas Dayton, founding president, Target

ROSEVILLE, MINNESOTA

The year 1962 was a turning point for the nation as well as the retail industry. The world was encroaching on an insular and parochial white America. Historical events and popular culture foreshadowed a schism between 1950s optimism and 1960s social unrest that would rupture into chaos later in the decade. While Jackie Kennedy was giving television crews a tour of the elegantly refurbished White House, President Kennedy was meeting behind closed doors with Martin Luther King Jr. to discuss civil rights. The Beach Boys released "Surfin' Safari," their paean to laid-back California beach culture; meanwhile, the soundtrack from "West Side Story," a remake of Romeo and Juliet set amid white-Puerto Rican gang wars in New York, soared to number one and stayed there for 54 weeks. John Glenn became the first American to orbit the earth, and in the same year, the United States experienced its first casualties in Vietnam, as well as the Cuban Missile Crisis.

The retail industry was on the verge of its own schism—between the establishment world of downtown department stores, and the more democratic discount operators, who had a hunch the glory years of their well-heeled counterparts had come and gone. In 1962, although the discount business generated more than $4 billion in revenue, it represented just 7 percent of all retail sales. The budding mass merchants were cheered on by new publications like *Discount Merchandiser*, which urged the industry to adopt the slogan "Sell more things to more people."[1] Target, Kmart, and Wal-Mart debuted in the year 1962, along with Kohl's, a Milwaukee-based discounter that still provides Target with stiff competition in apparel; and Crate & Barrel, a home store started by a couple, Gordon and Carol Segal, who had trouble finding affordable, stylish furniture for their Chicago apartment. But many downtown department stores had yet to feel the winds of change: Hudson's flagship, for instance, had two $1 million dollar sales days in 1962, outselling the suburban branches. In 1963, the founder's great-nephew Joseph L. Hudson Jr. took over and expanded the upscale offerings—serving champagne inside the store for the first time at the opening of the art gallery on the seventh floor, featuring works by Picasso, Jacques Lipschitz, and Enrico Donati.[2]

Dayton's planned and launched four Targets in the first year of operation—in Roseville, Crystal, Duluth, and Knollwood—all suburbs of Minneapolis-St. Paul. Douglas Dayton said his small team worked 80 hours a week preparing for the opening, and the division's nine buyers focused on stocking cutting-edge merchandise. "I remember when we told the [electronics] buyer we had to have FM radios in stock, and he didn't know what FM was," he said with a smile. Even then, Target buyers were adventurous, taking a gamble on innovative merchandise. The electronics buyer was also responsible for the "trim the tree" shop. "Everybody laughed at him when he brought in artificial [Christmas] trees," Dayton recalled. "They said, 'You can't sell artificial trees!' He was a great merchant. They sold."

The first Target opened on May 1 on a 20-acre site in Roseville, offering 65 percent hardlines, like auto supplies and appliances, 35 percent soft goods, such as clothing and accessories. The 68,800-sq.-ft. store even sold groceries, through a 25,000-sq.-ft. department leased to Applebaum's Food Market of St. Paul. The interior featured an innovative racetrack layout—still used today—and a courtesy desk smack in the middle of the store, ready to provide refunds in cash at any time, similar to George Draper Dayton's policy when he started his dry goods business. "We will offer high-quality merchandise at low margins because we are cutting expenses," Douglas Dayton told reporters at the opening. "We would much rather do this than trumpet dramatic price cuts on cheap merchandise. . . . we will ask ourselves where can we cut costs and how cheaply can we sell this product."[3] Roseville was the smallest of the four stores, because Target took over the space from another retailer. The others ranged in size from 122,500 sq. ft. to 132,900 sq. ft.

Although sales were strong at $11.4 million, Target lost $627,000 that year. Then Douglas Dayton discovered they had miscalculated their merchandise needs by a wide margin, and wound up with a $1 million overstock. The "bull's-eye clearance" was created out of necessity. "It took us until 1963 to get rid of it," said Dayton. "In 1964 we could buy what we wanted to and we started to roll." Sales rose to $27 million, and the stores showed a net profit of $630,000, giving the Dayton brothers the confidence to expand. But they took a more cautious approach than competitors like Kmart, which, although it had no discount retailing experience, signed leases for 33 stores, a total investment of $80 million, before it opened for business. "Their backs were to the wall because their [S.S. Kresge] stores were going down the tubes," Douglas Dayton said. "We weren't able to think that aggressively. It just wasn't in our makeup. We wanted to open one city at a time, originally." (Just eight years later, Kmart would be the largest discounter, with 417 stores and $1.68 billion in sales, compared with Target's 24 units and $200 million in sales.[4])

In 1965, the Daytons opened another Target in Bloomington, Minnesota, which scored $10 million in sales in its first year, as well as a store in Denver. The Denver store was rushed into business in December, when Douglas Dayton got word that a rival was trying to usurp Target's logo. Dayton and Minnesota regional manager Cliff Rice flew to Denver immediately. "We found a 20-foot store front, and the man leasing it said he could be there about 5:30 PM. We could see a nice interior with the help of the street lights," Doug Dayton wrote in the company newsletter, *On Target* (June 1968, Vol. 2, No. 6). "His key fit the back—he thought—so our first encounter with him was trying to pry the screen door off to get at the lock. This didn't work. But the store looked just like what we wanted—and besides it was available in the morning. Our opening inventory was $29 of sundries from Walgreen's." The first sale: a 49-cent toothbrush.[5]

That same year, Donald Dayton stepped down as chief executive of the corporation, handing the reigns over to his brother Bruce, but continuing to serve as chairman of the board until 1968. Meanwhile, Wallace Dayton decided it was time to move on as well. Since joining the company in the late 1940s, he had been vice president in charge of developing systems and controls, where he cut costs and modernized operations. He then became president of the Dayton Development Company, boosting profits at the company's two completed shopping centers, and overseeing one under construction. Wallace had an epiphany on a family trip to Alaska. "I wanted to do something on my own where I could really express myself," he told a reporter in 1979. "I'm lucky I had the money to do it."[6] He left the corporation to put his energies into environmental causes, later becoming national chairman of The Nature Conservancy.

Bruce Dayton, the new CEO, was the brother who always had a full wallet as a kid, ready to loan his brothers a few dollars when they needed cash—at a mere ten percent interest. He recalls sitting on his father's lap as a boy, discussing the differences among stocks, bonds, and mortgages. As a Yale undergrad he subscribed to the *Wall Street Journal*, even though he majored in English. So great was his interest in finance (and his dislike of merchandising), Bruce even quit Dayton's for a six-month period in the 1940s and explored working at a small investment company. But he returned to Dayton's, this time taking a job that better suited his skills, in the finance department.

In 1966, Bruce Dayton combined his love of literature and finance by launching B. Dalton Bookseller (named after him, with an *l* in place of the *y*). "It fit the demographics of the time—greater leisure, greater affluence, greater education," he said. "We had a very fine book department in (Dayton's), so we knew they were profitable." Most bookstores were mom-and-pop stores crying out for rationalization. B. Dalton's added computer inventory control and flashy marketing, and in short order became the largest hardcover bookstore in the United States. The chain grew to several hundred units before the company sold it to Barnes & Noble in 1986 for $85 million.

Donald had led his father's company into new businesses—malls, real estate development, and discount stores—with what has been described as "a blend of seat-of-the-pants daily decisions fortified with a sense for excellence and merchandising wisdom."[7] Bruce's management style was more formal; he liked to look long-range, incorporating five-year plans into the operations. He also shifted the performance benchmarks from measuring results and costs against the previous year's numbers, to measuring against specific goals. Bruce—the adolescent banker—also brought a profit focus to the firm, and developed strong financial disciplines to support Dayton's rapid growth. "One time a fellow from Goldman Sachs came in, and I said, 'Look, our sales are pretty good but our profits are not so hot.' And he said, 'Well that's what we expect from privately owned companies.' So we decided we didn't want to be just as good as a privately owned company, we wanted to be just as good as anyone could be. And so we tried lots of ideas; they didn't all work, but that didn't deter us. We just kept searching for the successful formula."

"CUSTOMERS STARTED CALLING IT *TARZHAY*"

Douglas Dayton was already convinced they had found the right formula. One day he strolled into Bruce's office and predicted Target would become a $100 million business. Both Bruce and Ken thought their brother was crazy, expecting the division to do perhaps $50 million a year. In 1968, when Target achieved the $100 million mark, Douglas raised his prediction to $1 billion. Although rivals like Kmart were expanding more quickly than Target, Douglas told executives at a 1968 celebration, "I am thoroughly convinced that we are producing a superior product which will bear the test of time."[8]

Douglas said capturing the niche of "upscale discounter" was key to Target's long-term success. "Duluth was the first place I heard it: Customers started calling it 'Tarzhay.' That was 1962," Douglas Dayton said. "When we had two stores in Hennepin County, 51 percent of the population shopped with us, a greater percentage than Southdale (mall) had. We surprised 'em, because they had such low expectations for a discount store. When you're in the department store business and you go out to parties, you hear about how the drapes are too long and the carpets are too late. People expected everything out of a department store. And we were surprising them with Target. They would exclaim about different features of it—assortments, prices—partly because they didn't have such a high level of anticipation." Target opened two more stores in Denver in 1966. By the end of that year, sales at the seven stores hit $60 million, and the chain was turning a profit. In 1967, another pair of stores opened in Minnesota, and Target employed 3,000 people. The company began eyeing St. Louis as its next frontier.

By the late 1960s, the Dayton brothers realized they needed more money for expansion, and decided to tap the public markets to finance their growth—although the Dayton family would remain majority owners after the offering. Bruce Dayton continued to press for professional management, bringing in four outside directors before the initial public offering: Stephen Keating, president of Honeywell; Robert Keith, chairman of The Pillsbury Company; David Lilly, president of Toro Manufacturing Corporation; and Philip Nason, president of The First National Bank of Saint Paul. The IPO involved four Dayton's department stores, nine Target stores, and a handful of B. Dalton bookstores and jewelry stores, which together produced $265 million in sales. A public offering of 450,000 shares was priced at $34 a share on October 18, 1967.[9] The prospectus noted that Dayton's would triple the number of Target stores over the next few years, and expand its markets beyond Minneapolis, Denver, and St. Louis. Dayton's put the money to work quickly: Between 1967 and 1971 it acquired 13 regional retailers, including upscale chains, discounters and specialty stores, and continued to expand the B. Dalton bookstore chain. Its boldest move, however, was the 1969 purchase of the larger J.L. Hudson Company of Detroit for $150 million in stock. Dayton's changed the company's name to Dayton Hudson, and by 1972, annual sales had mushroomed to $1.3 billion.[10]

A FALLING OUT, AND NEW COMPETITION

In the summer of 1968, as Target began work on two St. Louis stores, general manager John Geisse had a falling out with other executives over expansion plans. He contended that Target would get a better return on investment if it disregarded new markets and focused exclusively on saturating the suburbs of Minnesota, Denver, and St. Louis, where competition was less severe. Dayton's executives disagreed. While the St. Louis stores opened with the usual fanfare—Brenda Roberts, Miss St. Louis of 1968, was on hand to demonstrate kitchen gadgets—Geisse defected for The May Company. The department store was setting up its own discount chain, also in St. Louis, its hometown. "John went from Target [to The May Company] with the rolled-up blueprints of the chain under his arm—and the first Venture store was identical in layout," said former Target executive Norm McMillan. "He was disappointed he wasn't named president of [Target]." Media accounts say Geisse poached key executives; Douglas Dayton denies that, and wouldn't comment further on Geisse's departure. Geisse eventually left Venture, and in 1983 founded one of the first warehouse stores—the Wholesale Club of Indianapolis. By 1990, Geisse had expanded the chain to more than two dozen units in six Midwestern states with annual sales of about $650 million. That year he sold the chain for $163 million in stock to Wal-Mart, where he was already a board member and consultant. The Wholesale Club merged with Wal-Mart's Sam's Club division.[11] "I know [Geisse] was a real friend and confidante of Sam Walton. They were both kind of wild-eyed dreamers about retail and always willing to try something new," said former Hudson's executive Les Dietzman, who worked for Walton in the 1980s. "I know that he and Sam talked a lot about item merchandising, and things like that."

Despite Geisse's defection, Target continued to expand aggressively. In 1969, the discounter moved into Texas and Oklahoma with six stores, becoming a 17-store chain, and established a regional structure, with districts in St. Louis and Dallas. In 1970, Douglas Dayton moved on to senior vice president of administration for the parent company, Dayton Hudson. His earlier roles— starting the second department store in Rochester and then launching Target—had been entrepreneurial, and he missed the freedom to innovate and the thrill of running the stores every day. His new job required centralizing operations of the Target stores and the newly acquired divisions. "That was dullsville," he sighed. "Coming out of the stores, a corporate staff job was not interesting." After 22 years with Dayton's, he left. He headed up a venture capital firm, and supported conservation groups, the YMCA, and the Urban League. "Each of us moved on when we felt it was appropriate," Bruce Dayton said. "That was a different approach than most family businesses."

And then there were two. In 1970, Kenneth Dayton took over as CEO, while Bruce became chairman of Dayton Hudson. Ken loved the goods, rising through the merchandising side of the company. His sales experience dated back to his years as a student at the Blake School for Boys in Minneapolis, selling advertising for the yearbook.[12] While Bruce loved numbers, Ken was interested in building people, and focused his efforts on organizing solid talent to run the company. He developed a concept he called "organizational surplus": Every high-level manager would train a backup to replace him for the time when he moved into a higher position. "Kenny was a little better operator than I am, he was just better managing people," said Bruce. "We all realized our job was to develop a management team who could do it better than we did. Then we got out of the way and let them run it."

The Dayton brothers put such a high premium on developing talent, in fact, the human resources director of each company reported directly to the CEO. "The personnel organization at Dayton Hudson was very, very strong," explained former Target CEO Floyd Hall. "The feeling was that nothing was more important than the people . . . to identify new talent, retain people, develop the people you have, communicate. It was a very important structural change for a lot of corporations [the Daytons acquired]. And you can see the corporation does have outstanding people and communications skills with the people there now."

The J.L. Hudson Company, Detroit

In 1969, Dayton's purchased The J.L. Hudson Company of Detroit for $150 million in stock. Hudson's was larger than Dayton's, but the two had much in common: Both were downtown jewels, founded by religious, hard-working entrepreneurs who came from poor backgrounds; both differentiated themselves from the other dry goods dealers of the day with attention to service and price. Both built their flagship stores on sites formerly owned by the Presbyterian church, and forged ahead despite warnings from skeptics that their locations were too obscure. Both invested in training their workforce, and were deeply involved in their communities.

Joseph Lowthian Hudson, from England, with an eighth grade education, started working at 13 years old as a telegraph messenger boy and then a grocer's helper, a job that paid $5 a month.[13] Hudson's family moved to Pontiac, Detroit, where he and his father found jobs in a store owned by Christopher Mabley. When Mabley opened a branch store in Ionia, Michigan, the two men moved there to run it and eventually bought Mabley out, renaming the business R. Hudson & Son, and expanding it quickly. But the 1873 panic that had dashed George Draper Dayton's college aspirations left Joseph Hudson bankrupt, and his father died the same year. He paid his creditors 60 cents on the dollar, and returned to Detroit in 1877 to work for Mabley. By 1881, had saved enough money to open his own clothing store in the first floor of the Detroit Opera House.[14] Like George Draper Dayton, Joseph Hudson had a high sense of honor, and in 1888, sent checks to all of his former creditors for the additional 40 percent he owed them, plus commission.[15]

The competition between the J.L. Hudson Company and C.R. Mabley was as bitter as the Macy's-Gimbels rivalry in New York, with both sides taking out dueling full-page ads known as "shouting" advertisements. The ads lured crushing throngs of bargain hunters, gathering up their long, pleated skirts over the river of mud and horse manure in the unpaved streets.[16] Hudson's was among the first retailers to specifically price clothing, rather than bargaining, and to allow customers to return merchandise. By 1891, Hudson's was the largest retailer of men's clothing in the United States, and in 1906, the store's sales surpassed $1 million.[17]

Hudson, the entrepreneur, could not resist the opportunity to jump into Detroit's fledgling auto industry. In 1909, he partnered with seven others and invested $90,000 to produce a car and start a company that would bear his name. The Hudson Motor Car Company peaked in 1929, ranking third in the industry behind Ford and Chevrolet.[18] By 1910, Detroit was the ninth largest city in the United States, and in 1911, Hudson decided to expand his store. He had purchased an adjacent building, demolished it, and constructed a new ten-story structure of brick and terra cotta, attached to the original building through a series of passages.[19]

Like George Draper Dayton, Joseph Hudson valued his employees, and built a summer resort on a lake in Walkerville, Ontario, where female workers could come for two weeks at a time, free of charge. The new store itself had an employee lounge, a subsidized cafeteria, and an infirmary with a full-time nurse.[20] Unfortunately, Hudson didn't take as much care with his own health. Weighed down by the responsibilities of the store and the auto company, he sailed for England in 1912 to visit his homeland and rest. He caught pneumonia and just a week after his arrival, died at the age of 66.[21]

Hudson's five nephews, Robert Tannahill, and the Webber brothers—Richard, Oscar, Joseph, and James—took over the store, eventually expanding it to 25 stories stretching a city block. At its peak from the 1930s to the 1960s, the store—once the nation's tallest department store—had 12,000 employees and 100,000 customers a day. It was a truly a remarkable operation—"five basements, 51 passenger elevators, 17 freight elevators, 51 display windows, 706 fitting rooms, 2 million square feet, and 5,000 drafty windows," according to The *Detroit News*.[22] Hudson's boasted five restaurants, serving 14,000 meals per day, as well as carpentry shop, lending library, executive spa, and squash court. Elevator operators in smart uniforms ran the brass-door cabs and attendants offered ironed towels in the ladies' lounges. Hudson's sponsored the world's largest fireworks display on the Fourth of July, and a Thanksgiving Day parade (started in 1925) that rivaled the Macy's affair in New York. Its Christmas decorations and 12th floor Toyland were legendary.[23]

Ed Yager, a Utah consultant, worked for Hudson's throughout the 1960s. "I think the thing I enjoyed most about being there was the intense relationship that we had with customers," Yager recalled. "Hudson's had a thing that they called the 'Personal Order Board.' And at the time we used to brag about it—we had more operators on the Personal Order Board than they had at the Pentagon. Those were in the days when we didn't have computers—people sat at switchboards and acted as operators, and there were millions, millions of orders that went through that order board." Hudson's was also the Fed Ex of its time, delivering every package overnight in its fleet of 300 olive-green trucks. "If it didn't get there overnight, then one of us, as an executive, would pick it up and we would deliver it to make sure they had it the next day," said Yager. "The relationship with the customer was very, very, very intense. We look at Nordstrom today as the model, but I think Hudson's really preceded that with its intense customer relationship model."

An entire floor of Hudson's store was devoted to training. Ed Yager's sister, Esther, was a corporate training director in the women's merchandising department in the late 1950s. For 20 minutes every morning, training events were held in beautifully decorated rooms with comfortable chairs and ever-present coffee and donuts. "Every day there was something—whether there was a fashion change in men's division, or a new line of merchandise, (or a course on) taking accurate inventory. We would bring in someone to present it or present it ourselves," she said. Forty years after Esther Yager left the company, she found herself shopping in a Hudson's. "The woman taking care of me said, 'Did you used to train at Hudson's? We just loved that training—we looked forward to it so much.' I never had anybody say they loved training."

Les Dietzman worked at Dayton Hudson from 1967 to 1986 before joining Wal-Mart, and then founded his own chain, Family Christian Stores. "The training was spectacular in all positions," he said. "I guess I thought that's the way all retailers were. I come to find out Dayton's and Hudson's put special emphasis on training, and it has really served me well."

Yager said workers had a sense of pride about belonging to Hudson's—it was huge honor, for instance, to march in the Thanksgiving Day parade. "We had a common vision; we knew what we were and who we were and what was important," he explained. "And the sense of urgency around, for example, having the merchandise on the floor to cover an ad. I mean there was no question we would stay all night to have that merchandised marked and have it up to cover an ad on Tuesday morning. You'd find executives down in receiving room unpacking merchandise to get it out and get it on the floor. I don't know that you see that much anymore."

Hudson's in Crisis

In the late 1960s, while Dayton's celebrated its public offering and promising move into discounting, Hudson's was beginning to struggle. Suburban flight and the boom in malls had diverted the retail trade away from the nation's downtowns. According to one account, from 1948 to 1954, the downtown share of retailing fell by one-quarter in 13 of the nation's largest metropolitan areas, and the profit margins of downtown department stores tumbled lower than they had been even in the Depression.[24]

In 1966, a 30-year-old clerk and father of two was murdered in the store apprehending a shoplifter, who pulled a knife and stabbed him in the chest.[25] In the summer of 1967, the city's long-simmering racial tensions exploded in five days of rioting and looting. By the time the National Guard pulled out of Detroit, some 43 people were dead and more than 650 injured; property damage was estimated at $50 million.[26] By the time of the riots, three of the Webber brothers had died and the fourth, Joseph, died in 1970. Joseph L. Hudson, Jr., the grand nephew of the founder, had been named general manager of the store in 1957 at the age of 27. In 1969, as a generation of leadership passed away, he agreed to a merger with Dayton's of Minneapolis.

The combination created a national giant with department stores, discounters, and specialty stores, boasting $800 million in sales. "When the merger is complete," a Dayton official told *Discount Store News*, "we will acquire $138 million in equity capital from Hudson's and will be able to step up the expansion of our Target and Lechmere stores."[27] Hudson's 49-acre downtown icon never recovered from the continued suburban flight: It slowly eliminated services and closed departments, finally shutting its doors in 1983 after 102 years in business—although corporate headquarters remained there until 1990. Over the next eight years, vagrants took up residence in the abandoned building and vandals pillaged the store, stripping its regal marble, brass, and mahogany. "It was a personal hurt to everybody to see that happen," said former Hudson's manager Esther Yager. "For years it was like watching somebody being slowly tortured." In 1998, J.L. Hudson's flagship store came to a dramatic end: It was imploded with more than 2,700 pounds of explosives.[28]

Although the thrust toward professional management began in the mid-1960s, Bruce and Ken Dayton made it a top priority. They started a school of professional management with General Mills, Honeywell, and Northwest Bank (now Wells Fargo) to train department managers, "so that everyone in the company was singing the same tune," Bruce Dayton said. They polished the company's internal planning and control systems, and demanded critical feedback from the board of directors. The board was responsible for reviewing the CEO, and his bonus depended on the review. "Most of the CEOs who have gone out of line have been big egos that haven't been reviewed and haven't felt they were accountable to anybody," Bruce Dayton said. In 1974, when earnings floundered, Ken went so far as to ask the board if they wanted him replaced.

A *Harvard Business School* case study examined the company's unique system for reviewing the performance of the chairman and CEO. The CEO would do a self-evaluation first, based on objectives decided on the previous year, and then board members would rate his performance on how well he accomplished those objectives. His bonus was calculated from a combination of those ratings and the company's financial performance. David McLaughlin, a director in 1990, noted: "The board has got to make certain that there are objectives and goals for the company that are reflective of the interests of the stakeholders, and that the policies of the company are supportive of those goals, and that there's a commitment on the part of management to conduct the company in a way that's consistent with that. The board has critical stewardship over that process, and is responsible for it. But the board invests a huge amount of that responsibility in the CEO. . . . If the board acknowledges its responsibilities, and there are already clearly defined objectives of what the company is trying to do, then it must have a way of communicating clearly and honestly with the CEO, or the board will not be able to perform that function. To me, this [review] process fits in that matrix in a very critical way."[29]

Feedback and performance measurement extended all the way down to the management ranks. "Everyone who was a college graduate working at the professional level had written goals that were spelled out and agreed upon to accomplish during the year," explained Allan Pennington, former vice president of corporate development. "The manager then would write his pre-review and give it to his boss, and he would gather all of those; his boss would write his pre-review and it would go to the person above him, on up to the CEO, and the CEO would evaluate the people below him. The officers would get feedback from the boss and go review the people below them. The fiscal year began on February 1, so usually when those got nailed down and after results for company were in, you would be reviewed on previous year."

"We had a very good review system," Doug Dayton said. "I remember one guy had his final review okayed [by me], so I reported and his score got knocked down 5 points. It had about a thousand dollar effect on the bonus, and Dick complained about it. I thought I'd scored it right in the first place, but I went back and got it adjusted because I agreed with him. The way he scored himself, I concurred, was better."

While the Daytons established formal systems for orientation and training, employees also received informal coaching. "You want a good manager? Put him under a good manager and let him run the business," said Floyd Hall, Target chairman and CEO in the 1980s. "The best way to develop people is by osmosis. A person who has high performance standards trains people to have high performance standards. Mentoring is the critical part; obviously we had training tools and so on down the line—but they are not worth anything if you don't have someone constantly explaining what we stand for and how we do things."

In 1974, Bruce Dayton moved to chairman of the executive committee, and three years later left full-time management and became chairman of the board's finance committee. Ken met annually with the board's personnel committee to review the talent and a timetable for transition from the Daytons to non-family management. "We tried to develop a concept of excellence," Ken said in a magazine interview. "We thought a lot about the kind of business we wanted to run. We hoped we could develop, run, and turn over a corporation that would not only succeed but be exemplary."[30] In 1976, Ken became a director of the corporation, and William A. Andres was named chairman and CEO. It was a wise choice, said Floyd Hall. "Bill Andres was a guru when it came to strategic planning. He was a thoughtful, intelligent guy who required each company to go through the discipline. The whole strategic planning process was really ahead of its time." A master planner, Andres would make a strong impression on the executives who would later lead Target.

Andres also shared the Dayton brothers' modest disposition, a soft-spoken gentleman without an ounce of the arrogance that might come with running a 400-store corporation, said Alan Pennington. Pennington recalled the time Andres was walking through a Dayton's store and realized he had promised to return a phone call at 5 PM—and it was two minutes before. "So he just walked behind the cosmetics counter to make the phone call, and the lady behind the counter just about had a heart attack," Pennington related. "She said, 'You can't be back here, you can't use this phone, get out of here!' He introduced himself as the CEO of company and she was totally embarrassed and wanted to hide. And he said,

'Don't be embarrassed, you did exactly what you were supposed to have done. There's no reason to know who I am by sight, and I was wrong for not telling you who I was and that I wanted to use the phone.' In addition, he wrote a letter to her supervisor telling him what good job she had done. He also sent her flowers and called the internal house newsletter and suggested she be featured in the next newsletter."

After Douglas Dayton and John Geisse left Target, William Hodder was named president. The Daytons created a task force of middle managers to devise a growth strategy for Target for the next five to fifteen years.[31] "In this constantly changing business," Hodder told *Discount Store News*, "you can never be satisfied with the present methods, as successful as they may be. As we expand into more and more markets, we'll need ever more sophisticated methods at both the headquarters and at the store level. This comprehensive task force study should help us stay ahead of the game."[32]

But Target's game plan for growth turned out to be overly ambitious. Through new stores and converted acquisitions, Target grew to 46 stores by 1972, and the combination of overexpansion, higher remodeling costs, and management turnover led to a drop in profits. The chain also discovered its department store heritage could be a disadvantage: At the time, discounters changed over merchandise faster than traditional department stores, and Target didn't keep pace. It also continued to control product buys at headquarters, resulting in some memorable flubs: snow shovels showing up in Tulsa, Oklahoma; ski suits designed for Minnesota's sub-zero temperatures going begging in Denver stores; and Walleye lures showing up in Houston. While there is plenty of good fishing in the Gulf of Mexico, there aren't any Walleyes.[33]

In 1973, Stephen Pistner was named chairman with a mission to restore profitability, along with senior vice president Kenneth Macke, who would eventually become chairman and CEO. As part of the revitalization of Target, a new group of executives came together to design an identity and strategy based on the principles that had guided Dayton Hudson since the turn of the century. In the next chapter, we'll review the strategic planning methods, and a blueprint called *Guides for Growth*, which Target continues to follow today.

◎ CHECK OUT

Management Excellence

Long-range planning: The Daytons incorporated five-year plans into the operations, and polished the company's internal planning and control systems.

Tougher benchmarks: The Daytons shifted the performance benchmarks from measuring results and costs against the previous year's numbers, to measuring against specific goals. They also put a stronger focus on profit, developing strong financial disciplines to support rapid growth.

Critical feedback: The brothers brought in four outside directors in the 1960s, and demanded honest feedback on the company's performance. They made the board responsible for reviewing the CEO, which determined his bonus.

Training, development, and coaching: The Daytons started a school of professional management with General Mills, Honeywell, and Northwest Bank (now Wells Fargo) to train managers. Ken Dayton developed a concept called "organizational surplus," in which every high-level manager would train a backup to replace him for the time when he was promoted to a higher position. Dayton's made developing talent a priority by having the human resources director of each company report directly to their CEOs. Employees received informal coaching as well; they were matched with mentors who explained what the company stood for and how things were done.

Systematic performance reviews: Employees and their bosses would agree upon certain performance objectives for the year, and this provided the basis for year-end reviews. The employee did a self-evaluation and was then reviewed by his boss, and bonus compensation was based on the performance review.

CHAPTER 9

Guides for Growth

In retail there are lots of ways to be
marginally crooked, and we decided we
weren't going to do that.

—Norman McMillan, former vice president
of strategic planning, Target

LAYING THE FOUNDATION

The Dayton Brothers, with Douglas Dayton at the helm, closely guided Target's entrepreneurial years. But by the early 1970s, Douglas had returned to the parent company, and merchandising guru John Geisse had defected for The May Company to start the discount chain Venture. Dayton's attention was focused on digesting its merger with department store J.L. Hudson, as well as more than a dozen specialty retailers it acquired after its public offering. Target experienced its own growth spurt, acquiring 16 stores from New York-based Arlans in 1972. Some stores were smaller and less uniform than the standard Target stores, and so required more time to devise the right merchandising formula. At the same time, overall costs were rising, sales were declining and the company lacked experienced talent to handle the sudden expansion to 46 stores.

"From 1962 to 1969 Target did very well and then fell off the charts for two to three years," noted Allan Pennington, former vice president of corporate development for the Dayton Hudson Corporation. Target's new president, William Hodder, was a former IBM executive heavily focused on technology. "His philosophy was, 'Just give me the computer printouts and I can sit in my office and run this company,'" Pennington said. "It proved to be so far from the truth it was incredible. While he was paying attention to the computer sheets, nobody was paying attention to customers and merchandising." Meanwhile, lacking oversight from the top, Target's 46 store managers began to run things their own way. "The company was worshipping at the altar of individualism," recalled Norman McMillan, Target's vice president of strategic planning at the time. "Remember, the time period is about two years after Earth Day. It was not uncommon to walk in the store, and a store manager would have hired a carpenter and nailed wooden shingles along a whole wall because he thought it would look good. There was stuff like that going on all over the chain. Our job was to put that energy into selling product."

The revitalization that took place in the 1970s turned out to be one of the most critical periods in Target's history. Executives took the nascent values and strengths of an entrepreneurial company and codified them, created systems to support them, and consciously crafted a culture that would carry the company into a more mature phase. The Dayton brothers assembled a new team led by Stephen Pistner, a Dayton Hudson group vice president who had sold his specialty chain, Team Electronics, to Dayton Hudson. Kenneth Macke was named senior vice president, merchandise manager of soft lines.

In Pistner, the Daytons found a dynamic, colorful, and informal leader who assembled an unusual crew to carry out his mission. "I was attracted to strong individual personalities—combined with an agreement between us that you'll meet your objectives and goals," he said. "I managed with a loose hand as long as they delivered. Your order to me is, 'I'll do it my way.' If you can tolerate that—and being told to go screw yourself more times than you want to hear—that makes a company unique, and eventually delivers the highest profits."

Norman McMillan, for example, "was unmanageable," Pistner said. "The only person who could manage Norm McMillan was Norm McMillan. The first day on the job he pulled his glasses up to the top of his head—he had this shock of white hair—and he said, 'I can't see any reason why the hell I'd like to work for you.' I looked at him and said, 'Well, Norman, that's an interesting way to start.' He said, 'Everybody wants to be a super executive, to look good, and nobody wants to get anything done.' I said, 'Tell people what you want. What's the course and destiny of the company? Then teach them what that means.' That became Norman's responsibility."

McMillan and the new executive team outlined Target's identity, operating environment, and goals in a document called *Guides for Growth*. The manifesto contains about a dozen statements of strategy, which laid the foundation for the kind of company Target would become—principles that are plainly apparent in the way the chain does business today. "Norman's work was so good, it became one of those documents read throughout the retail industry," said Pistner. "In all my years in business, I don't remember a better document to guide a business by. People who worked at Target knew who they were when they read the document."

Guides for Growth was developed in a series of meetings led by McMillan, in which the team argued through what Target would stand for. "The meetings were turbulent, there were expressions of all kinds, it was a wild place, but everybody had a chance to make a contribution, and we understood we had to go in single direction," Pistner recalled. None of the Dayton brothers participated in the strategy sessions, presumably because they were occupied elsewhere—but as a result the Target team owned the plan and were invested in implementing it. That's not to say the planning process was a touchy-feely exercise in corporate unity. "They said in effect, 'You guys develop a strategy, you do it,'" McMillan noted. "It was sort of, do it, or everybody goes. Strategic planning is not done when things are going well. It's done when there's fear in the air and you expect to lose your job."

The document laid out 10 to 12 major principles that were stated in single sentence, then elaborated on them. "We spelled out in detail what each meant, and that detail was the key to success," Pennington said. "If you take a look at the one-sentence strategy, it could apply to most any company. But spelling out what that means, and that Target was committed to it, made the difference. I'm sure it's been modified over what it was then, but based on what I see in the stores, they're still following the basics of it."

Strategic Planning

The process Target stores went through to develop *Guides for Growth* was happening corporation-wide at Dayton Hudson in the 1970s. The company had about a dozen different divisions, and each went through the discipline of building its own comprehensive strategic plans. "In 1973, it was very common among all industries to believe in having a strategic planning department," said former Target chairman and CEO Floyd Hall. "But Dayton Hudson believed in each company having its *own* strategic plan. It makes sense to have the people closest to the business decide which direction the company should take, much more than some guy in an office smoking a pipe and coming up with a grand plan."

Hall said 15 to 18 key executives would meet offsite for three days, and discuss company identity, external threats, and external opportunities, as well as internal weaknesses and strengths. "We would talk about what the company was going to stand for—if you were going to be the upscale discounter, well, what do you mean?" Hall explained. "That question would get asked so everyone knew exactly what the company was trying to do, and what the company would stand for in terms of image, service, product offering, cleanliness, and so on.

"External threats might be the economy, unions, it could be the expansion of a new competitive strategy," he noted. "External opportunities might mean new strategies—a warehouse club . . . incorporating the Internet in your stores. Then you turned to internal weaknesses—what things internally were keeping the company from really performing better? Was it a breakdown in logistics, were your distribution systems sufficient, were you moving products rapidly at low cost, did the systems support the kind of information buyers needed to make decisions, were you being good to your people, and were your people in the stores helpful? Then we would look at internal strengths—what do we do well, what can we do better, and how go about doing it? It was critically important in developing a strategic plan to position the company against its competition, and make it a better company."

Once issues were identified under one of the four umbrellas (internal weakness, external weakness, internal strength, external strength), the executives would develop a "corrective plan of action" or an "opportunity plan of action," and then assign the task to the senior officers responsible, whether in merchandising, distribution, finance, or operations. "Because the environment involved identifying problems, you sometimes had a lot of squabbling, as you can imagine—everyone wanted to pick on someone else's area of expertise," Hall noted. "That's okay, it helped strengthen the business. The important thing is when you leave, you have identified and farmed out tasks to the responsible people." Those people were then compensated and rewarded on their progress in solving problems or capitalizing on opportunities. "There's no better way to get their attention than to tie it to their wallets," explained Hall. "You would have personal objectives assigned off the strategic plan—the guy who ran distribution would have five personal objectives beyond his financials. He got 25 percent of his bonus based on his ability to deliver improvements on his strategic objectives; the other 75 percent was based on financial performance."

The CEO's incentives were structured in the same manner. "You were graded as a chief executive on the quality of your strategic plan—which affected your compensation and the bonus you got at the end of the year," Hall continued. "In addition, each corporation had detailed financial goals and you would measure against those. At the end of the year you would sit down with somebody in corporate and they would give you a fair evaluation of your performance—you got a nice bonus or a pink slip. There's not a lot of ambiguity in retail."

Meanwhile, the quality of the strategic plan determined how much money a division would receive to build new stores, hire new managers, and fund its growth. "Basically the entire corporation ran on what I call a 'wheel of fortune,'" Hall explained. "Money was allocated to a company based on the quality of the strategic plan. To grow you needed new stores and capital, and all the money came based on how well they thought you could do what you said you were going to do. This was very important, because without money you don't grow."

Pennington, who initiated the capital allocation process, said when he started with the company, the officers would approve each division's strategy, then add up the cost. When it was too high, every division would have to go back and alter its strategic plan. Pennington changed the process so that each division presented its strategy with the cost. Then at the corporate level, the treasurer and controller could determine the total investment and return on capital, and present a comprehensive plan to the board. Then the whole package could be tweaked, rather than having each division start from scratch.

"It was politically difficult to get there," Pennington recalled. "I had trouble because the treasurer said, 'I don't want to make recommendation to top management' and the controller said, 'Don't get us involved with top management' and I said 'What the hell do you think our job is? Our job is to make their job easier.' So we could come in and say, the three of us are agreed on this package."

The Target division was particularly enthusiastic about the process, Pennington said. "There was a culture within Dayton Hudson and each company had its own culture. Target was the one that did the most work, and the best work, in creating strategic guides for growth," he said. "Others in the corporation thought of it as a requirement they had to get over to get money to build new stores. In Target they really believed in it, and took a lot of time to come up with these things."

The strategic planning process is ingrained at Target Corporation, Hall noted: "They would never think of changing it. The best gauge of performance is history. You're always going to change something, but it's really more modifying it. Dayton Hudson made a lot of modifications along the way because the industry was changing; you do things differently when you're running 800 stores versus 300. You may have to make changes, but you never fall from the basic principles."

HONESTY IS THE FIRST POLICY

Among the first decisions was that Target would be an "honest-dealing" store. "In retail there are lots of ways to be marginally crooked, and we decided we weren't going to do that," McMillan explained. "We [wanted] to shoot fair and square with customers—when we say something, we're going to mean it, and not only that, but take the next step." It took two days of debate to define this standard of honesty and figure out how it would be implemented. One aspect related to product quality. "We said we would offer good quality products sold at good prices," McMillan recalled. "That sounds like what everybody says, but it's not what everybody does. It's the way you have to execute on a piece of strategy."

Quality meant numerous rounds of testing, and sacrificing profits on products that didn't make the cut. Target's team knew if they committed to quality, word of mouth would follow. "By god, we tested living hell out of our stuff, not only in labs, but with our people," Pistner recalled. "People would notice, and customers would say, 'I bought that at Target.'" McMillan described the way Kenneth Macke, who later became president and CEO, acted on the code. A shipment of shoes that went into stores subsequently failed tests at a quality control lab. "I remember Ken Macke calling on the divisional merchandise manager, who said, 'I can't take these out [of the stores], this will cost us $75,000.' And Ken says, 'Okay, I'll tell you what you do. I want you to go out of the room and call every single store that has those shoes, and I want them taken out and thrown in the dumpster.' The guy blanched and turned white. And the point of that little episode is that people began to realize within Target that we were serious about quality."

Honest advertising was another way Target implemented the strategy. The decision was evocative of George Draper Dayton's 1903 policy of giving $1 to a shopper finding an error in a Dayton's ad, as well as his son's decision not to advertise goods that were more than 50 percent off—because he wanted ads to be not only true, but also credible. "If you read a lot of advertising today there's always the small print that's either there or inferred," Pennington explained. "Target said if it says the price is going to be such to such, then that's what it's going to be. A lot of companies will put a fantastic price on an item and only have six of them. Hundreds of people show up and then you've got them in the store. That's not illegal, but it's not honest. We monitored to make sure none of the stores were playing those games. When we ran ads we had the merchandise to back it up—and we had a raincheck policy so we would give the same price when we got the item back in."

Company officials decided accounting would be another aspect of the Target's honest-dealing ethic. "When we accounted for the money we spent, we accounted for it very conservatively. We never tricked ourselves or investors or anybody else," McMillan noted. For instance, other stores would hold a grand opening and amortize the advertising costs over a long time period. "At Target, if we opened a store, the advertising was charged to that day, so we were always current. There were no surprises."

Pennington said the value Target placed on honesty was a particular legacy of the Dayton family. "The Dayton brothers did everything morally, ethically, and culturally exactly the way it should have been done, and I can't emphasize that enough, particularly in today's world of Enron and Worldcom and all of that," he said. "There was nothing like that going on. It is a very, very honorable company." Target's decision to be a truthful operator is continuing to pay off today, said consultant Fred Crawford, coauthor of *The Myth of Excellence: Why Great Companies Never Try to Be the Best At Everything* (Crown Business, 2001). His theory: People are so hungry for basic human values they will flock to companies that provide it. For his book, Crawford surveyed consumers about specific business values. Some 84 percent said honesty was the most important quality a business could have—but only 15 percent believed businesses were honest. "Talk about a values chasm," Crawford remarked. "Here [honesty] is the most important thing, and everyone collectively believes businesses are dishonest. That's why Target—which does make us feel good [about its practices]—has a huge advantage."

STYLE AND FAMILY VALUES

As they debated the course of the company back in 1973, executives also reiterated the retailer's original aspiration—that Target would be the discount store with style. "You can sell stuff that's good quality and you can sell it cheap—but if it's not in style, it's not a good buy for customers and they know it," McMillan said. One component of that strategy was a decision to keep the company's headquarters in downtown Minneapolis rather than moving to cheaper office space on the outskirts, so buyers would see what the most fashionable customers were wearing. "That became a differentiator—just an edge—that there would be a stylishness to what we do, and the way we [maintain] the stores. Today, if you shop at Target, you'll find that compared to Kmart and Wal-Mart, the stores are cleaner," McMillan said. Target executives, in fact, obsessed about the floors. "We must have spent years figuring out how to get cleaner floors," said Macke, in an interview published a few years after *Guides for Growth* was completed. A St. Louis store manager finally developed the right combination of chemicals and muscle to do the job, and soon the formula was used in every store. "Shiny floors may seem like a very small point, but maybe not to a working woman or housewife who thinks she deserves a clean place to shop in," Macke said.[1]

Next, the architects of *Guides for Growth* decided Target would serve a specific demographic: young families. Target was quickly challenged on the decision by parents who called complaining about adult publications sold in the magazine section. O.C. Adams, senior vice president for store operations, "came back to a Target meeting and said, 'How can we have *Playboy* and *Penthouse*? That's not consistent if Target is a store for young families,'" Pennington recalled. "And somebody said, 'Well the reason we have them is we make a high profit on them, hundreds of thousands a year, and they take up little space.' And O.C. Adams said, 'In that case, why don't we amend the *Guides for Growth* and say, Target is a store for young families, except for the adult magazines.' Of course, everyone agreed it was inconsistent and we took them out of the stores." McMillan estimated that at that time, Target sold at least $1 million in *Playboy* and *Penthouse* magazines annually. "It was regarded as a very prudish move by others in the industry," he recalled. "But those magazines are out of discount stores altogether now. That got us a lot of publicity—and we thought it was good publicity: Target was a store for young families, and we took it seriously." Innovations over the years have focused on the family. Target was one of the first stores to make browsing with small children convenient, by offering ingenious shopping carts that could be attached to a two-seater cart, accommodating three kids.

OPERATIONAL AND PEOPLE STRATEGIES

While Target executives decided what the company stood for, Pistner and Macke got down to the nitty-gritty of solving operational problems. They were legion. "Customers would come up to front lanes and find long lines," Pistner explained. "It took enormous amounts of time to get through because there weren't tickets on all the merchandise, and customers would leave their baskets and walk out. The front counters looked terrible and couldn't handle all the bags." Macke, in his typical forthright style, performed his own engineering test. "He took his cart loaded with things and rammed it against the counter, and practically knocked it down," Pistner recalled, laughing.

Pistner's solution to the front of the store problems was emblematic of his business philosophy: He went straight to the front lines. "One day, secretly and quietly, I called together the ten top front-end managers—the women who ran the front of store—and told them to call in sick. I called them into the room and said, 'Ladies we're in deep trouble. I need your best answers to make things work in the front of the store, and your bosses can't give it to me. They said, 'Will you protect us?' I said, 'If you solve the problem, not only will I guarantee your jobs, I'll give you all a raise. And word will get out across the chain, and everyone will operate the way you say we should.' In three hours those women put out a list of ten things necessary to accomplish the mission and clean up the stores. We put out the list with orders to all field officers to implement it in 24 hours, and if they didn't implement it, their jobs would be at stake. Within 30 days the store operations were running clean. Word went out to the entire company how the job was done—not from the bosses but from [the front line]. The truth about business is that the people inside the business know how to make it work, and often the problem is in executives above. The answers are with the people."

In order to get more of those answers, Pistner did *walkarounds* as he called them, at least three days a week, asking people in every department what should be done to make the business better. His assistant, company veteran B.J. Gersey, whose discretion had won her the trust of her peers, steered Pistner in the right direction. "She would deliver messages telling me where we were going wrong and what I needed to do," Pistner recalled. "Within a year people thought I could smell trouble in a minute. It wasn't me, it was B.J. She would smell out the problem and alert me."

Pistner encouraged executives to do their own walkarounds, as well as something he called "slice of pie" management. For instance, an executive would find a problem in the computer system—the information wasn't carrying through to the inventories. "Someone would say, 'We have to go back to data centers and clean up the reports.' I said, 'Don't do that; take your report, walk through the company and ask each person at each level until you end up with Charlie on the loading dock. Find out what doesn't work. On this one little problem, we would find out what was wrong and resolve the problem throughout the company. Every woman and man you came in contact with could say, 'They asked me what was wrong and how to correct it. The report changed, and my idea is right there.' Then they had ownership to cleaning up the problem. You have to have every person you can touch be part of the success. If you print those words it sounds like bullshit. But if you really see a change in the way trucks are loaded, to ease the way in which the store unloads them, and Charlie says he know where that came from—it's real. It isn't Harvard management style, but walkaround management is clearly necessary to success. People communicate what's right, and you bring it back up the ladder and make sure it's done."

Pistner also motivated workers by creating heroes at each level of the company. "We determined where there were very solid, competent employees and then gave them a task—one we knew they would be capable of doing, but if they really worked their heart out, they could exceed very big. We gave them the opportunity, and then out of their success we would announce winners and promote them. You would then have the feeling that promotion was based on capability and accomplishment. They [began] to understand what success is and that they could each be in the glow of that success. I wouldn't tell Macke what to do; each person must achieve by himself and be looked upon as one of the group contributing to the main success of the company. It's not profound in any way, it's as basic as breathing, but it was real."

TECHNOLOGY, PRESENTATION, MERCHANDISING, AND GUARANTEES

As Pistner and Macke revamped operations, *Guides for Growth* laid out essential principles here, too. First, Target executives made a conscious decision that the chain would be committed to growth and developing cost-saving operational efficiencies, but would be the *second fastest* in the introduction of new technology, rather than first. It was a reaction to the legacy of Bill Hodder, the former Target president and IBM executive who put a priority on computer systems. But even before Hodder led Target, the chain had always strived for cutting-edge technology: In 1966 it installed a computerized payroll system to serve the chain. As early as 1970, it produced daily reports on what had sold in stores, and in 1972 it began testing electronic point-of-sale terminals. "There was such a strong culture in Target to be first at everything technological. A store manager may not know about running a store, but knew a hell of a lot about computers," McMillan explained. "We said we'd continue to be strong, but wouldn't let our stores be laboratories for IBM. That sounds like Target is anti-technology but it shouldn't be taken that way at all." Target, in fact, has become a leader in retail technology. (See Chapter 5.)

The architects of *Guides for Growth* stated that Target stores would be uniform throughout the chain, the first step in reigning in rebel store managers and centralizing decision-making to control costs. Former Target chairman and CEO Floyd Hall put it this way: "Target had the mentality that said, 'We will get a world class buying organization in place and let them make buying decisions and hold them accountable.' The store people would receive the goods and put them out and make sure they were priced right and get the store clean—all the operations responsibilities. And believe me, that's enough—you don't need store people making advertising and merchandising decisions."

That was around the time Pistner decided to paint the town red. "One of the things that was always said in department stores was 'We must blend, the colors must be soft, inviting, the merchandise cannot fight with the wall, everything should be bland.' I hired a designer and said we're going to become the most unique store in retailing. We did a design using a bright red color on the walls and the trim—bright red for the carts, running along the floor. I mean it was the most disastrous thing in the minds of retailers that you could do. When Ken Dayton heard about this I was told I'd probably be fired. We came down to Texas to test the store—and almost no customers mentioned that it was red. They said it was bright, fun to shop in and of course tied in with good merchandise and service. It was enormously successful as we moved the design throughout the country—and of course within five years, every store in discounting tried to copy it."

Stephen Pistner, Kenneth Macke and O.C. Adams subsequently conducted a systematic study of Target's floorplan, and in 1974 opened a new 100,000-sq. ft. prototype. A year later, the team introduced a "planogram," a formula that dictated exactly how the stores should be laid out. Over the years, the company has measured sales and margin per linear square foot, ranking the store from most to least profitable. That helps determine which areas are allotted more space, and which are cut back in size.[2] "Target was one of the first companies to embrace the planogram," Pennington noted, adding that headquarters relied on the map to create a uniform look throughout the chain. "For instance, they will periodically send out photographs and descriptions of exactly how a store should look. In health and beauty aids, it would [dictate] that you need the largest bottle of Finesse to the left, go three bottles wide, then the next four wide, and under that another kind of shampoo. Or, this goes on fixture 126 and here is exactly how fixture 126 is supposed to look. Now every store is not going to be exactly the same, but it's going to be real close."

Today, Target still follows a formal merchandising strategy designed to maximize profits. Les Dietzman, a Dayton Hudson executive for 20 years, left the company in 1986 to join Wal-Mart, and has seen both sides of the planning coin. "It starts with, let's look at all the things that are available to us, how much can we carry, what do we think the potential for sales of this department is, how are we going to present it? It's very well thought out and it's all calculated to get this kind of a turn, this kind of a margin," Dietzman explained. "I don't think the planning of Wal-Mart is as rigorous. It's more, 'How much can we sell, and does it look like we're going to sell more than that—well then, let's buy more.' It's just two different approaches to the same thing and they both have outstanding performance."

Former chief executive Floyd Hall said the planogram helped Target remain disciplined in its merchandising decisions. "The planogram was also the buyer's responsibility," Hall explained. "If a buyer wanted to buy three new models of a television or blender, they would have to kill three old ones. By giving the buyer full responsibility for the planogram, you were able to control what could otherwise be a haphazard buy, buy, buy—the thinking that, maybe if you buy three more, you'd get another sales counter."

Finally, the *Guides for Growth* team hashed out "a guarantee customers could understand," McMillan recalled. "It said something like, 'If you are ever disappointed or displeased with anything you purchase, bring it back and we'll give you your money back.' We posted that above the return desk in every Target store, and we also posted it at the cash register, so that the customer could see it. If she was having a discussion about bringing something back, the customer could say to the clerk, 'What about that guarantee over your head there?' So the customer was empowered to enforce the guarantee. It was another example of how the department store heritage came right on through. I think that was a very powerful thing, because in the 1970s, discount stores were not believed to carry merchandise as good as department stores, so the appearance of this guarantee in Target was an important difference." Recently, Target modified its return policy so that a receipt must accompany every return, and if the product is marked down in the meantime, the customer receives the reduced amount upon return. The new policy has disgruntled some customers—particularly those who use Target's bridal or baby gift registries. (See Chapter 5.)

SELLING GUIDES FOR GROWTH

Once *Guides for Growth* was finalized, Norman McMillan and the other officers signed at the bottom to underscore their commitment, and help sell the concepts to store staff. "A lot of people make decisions in the retail chain and we wanted them to know their boss was at the top and signing," he said. "Then we got kind of enamored of the idea of enforcing [the Guides]. We decided to do a road show, and talk first to officers, and then department heads and then regional managers, and then store managers and buyers. Then all the people in the chains would know about *Guides for Growth* and what we stood for. And we said, 'If you see us, the officers, deviating from this policy, we want you to stand up and yell.' People would come in and say, 'You said this in *Guides for Growth* and I don't think this is an example of that.' They were empowered to yell and that really worked."

Pennington recalled a time in which Kenneth Macke made his commitment to *Guides for Growth* abundantly clear. "Target held a meeting with all the store managers in the country. One of the assignments in breakout groups was to come up with specific examples of how *Guides for Growth* was *not* being followed, so management could stay on top of it," Pennington related. "The first guy stood up and said, 'In our group, *Guides for Growth* is followed 100 percent and we think they're fabulous.' And Ken Macke said, 'I think you must be the stupidest group out there, because I know that's not true. We're looking for growth here, not compliments.'" It was a blunt reply, but one that made management's desire for honest feedback crystal clear.

In addition to developing *Guides for Growth*, Target halted its expansion to just one store, and took huge markdowns to clear out inventory. By 1975, Target's turnaround strategy bore fruit: Sales grew 20 percent to $511 million, making it the corporation's number two profit-producer.[3] Back on target, the discount chain embarked on the path to growth once more—in just four years it would double sales, and vault to the number one division in sales at Dayton Hudson.

"When we got together and started running the company, 'Tarzhay' was a misnomer," Pistner said. "It had dirty floors and incompetent people taking care of it. I said, 'If I hear it referred to as Tarzhay, you're in serious trouble. You can call it Tarzhay again when you solve problems and it's worthy of the name.' Finally when the customers were happy, the stores were clean and profitable, we said, 'Now you can call it Tarzhay.' You have to work toward goals people find exciting, not this malarkey of managing behind closed doors in tall buildings."

"There was an excitement about the accomplishments the company was making," Pennington recalled. "It was fun to go to work every day. You were challenged to do your best. When I came in 1972, Dayton Hudson was kind of a mediocre company. They weren't a bad company, but they were not on the tip of everyone's tongue when they talked about who are the greatest retailers in America. Over time, management kept pushing: How can we raise the bar? How can we go to the next level? And over time the company just got better and better and better. By 1981 Dayton Hudson was probably among the best retailers in America, and it was really fun being on that ride, from a mediocre company to the best."

Pistner agreed. "There is no way to express the quality of that team in how hard they worked and how free they felt to make a business run well. We had a blast. It was this melding of individual, highly competent people, where everyone had full range of expression. It was a thrill to work in the company, a thrill to be able to say you were part of Target, and that went throughout the whole organization. And when you have growth and profit, you have jobs and the ability to promote people—no one else can compete with you."

Target would continue its winning streak, growing earnings every year for the next decade. In the meantime, through its customer-centric culture and generous philanthropy, the corporation would build enormous reserves of loyalty and goodwill—reserves it would have to tap to fight off a bruising takeover attempt.

⊙ CHECK OUT

Guides for Growth

Honest dealing: Target would shoot fair and square with customers; offer quality products at good prices; and be truthful in its advertising and accounting. (The chain offered a money back guarantee, since revised.)

Chic: Target would offer fashionable merchandise and maintain clean, stylish stores. The company kept its headquarters downtown rather than moving to the city's edge, so store buyers would be exposed to fashion-forward consumers.

Aimed at young families: Target would be oriented to serve young families; executives eliminated the profitable adult magazine section, offered kid-friendly shopping carts.

Focused on operations: Executives decided the chain would be committed to growth and developing cost-saving operational efficiencies, but would not allow technology to overshadow operations. Stores would be uniform in appearance and offerings, and goods purchased according to a planogram that maximized profitability.

Open to critical feedback: Target encouraged workers at all levels to identify problems and then implemented recommended changes. The feedback helped the store address trouble spots, stay true to its mission and become more profitable. Employees were rewarded based on their accomplishments.

CHAPTER 10

Philanthropy

The Foundation should live for centuries.

—George Draper Dayton, 1918

AN ACT OF FAITH REWARDED

In the spring of 1987, an anonymous investor began steadily acquiring Dayton Hudson stock. For a remarkable 15 years in a row, the Minnesota retailer, now the nation's seventh largest, had grown profits from continuing operations. But its other divisions couldn't make up for a disastrous 1986 at Mervyn's, where operating profits plummeted 35 percent. As a whole, Dayton Hudson posted $310 million in net income that year—a record—but more than a quarter of it came from the sale of B. Dalton bookstores to Barnes & Noble. The stock slipped to $42 a share in the second quarter of 1987, from $58.50 a year earlier.

In June 1987, shares of Dayton Hudson soared nearly $6 on heavy volume, amid speculation that someone was building a significant stake in the retailer—signaling the launch of a hostile takeover. Merger and acquisition activity was rife across the industry. Even though business had picked up and the outlook for profits was sunny, retailing stocks were cheap—still recovering from recession earlier in the decade. Meanwhile, many companies held valuable chunks of real estate that made them tempting takeover targets. Ample financing—in the form of pension funds and junk bonds—made it lucrative for corporate raiders to buy the chains, dismantle their assets and peddle them one by one (an era forever immortalized by director Oliver Stone's film "Wall Street").

Dayton Hudson was caught unawares. "We simply believe there's a hostile takeover because our stock has moved so fast," company chairman Kenneth Macke told the *Minneapolis Star Tribune.* "We don't know who."[1] The culprit was soon unveiled: the Dart Group, a Maryland-based operator of discount bookstores and auto supply stores run by Herbert Haft and his son Robert— dubbed "the most feared family in retailing" by *Fortune* magazine.

From a single storefront in Washington D.C., Herbert Haft built the Dart Drug chain, an empire boasting $283 million in revenue when he sold it in 1984. A pair of real-life Gordon Gekkos, father and son then gunned down six different takeover targets, selling their holdings for multimillion-dollar profits.[2]

In mid-September, when the Hafts finally weighed in with a $65 a share, $6 billion merger proposal, speculators swarmed. Within weeks, a third of Dayton Hudson's stock was owned by investors who had been shareholders for less than a month.[3] Dayton Hudson rejected the offer as inadequate, and a few days later, Dart upped the bid to $68 a share.[4]

The retailer scrambled to fend off the attack. "I was sitting in the CEO's office with the geniuses who know about this, and they tell us the stuff we're supposed to do in New York," recalled Peter Hutchinson, former head of government relations and the Dayton Hudson foundation. "And one of us said, 'Wait a minute, that means playing their game, with their rules, on their court. We're a Minnesota-based company and built a reputation in this community we think is valuable. Let's change the game.'" At the time, Dayton Hudson was Minnesota's largest company in terms of sales and employed 34,000 state residents. There were reasonable fears that Dart would sell or spin off parts of the retailer to pay for the mammoth deal, slashing jobs along the way.

Company officials decided to ask the state legislature to make a buyout more difficult. "I remember I got the CEO out of bed, we drove to a hotel in downtown Minneapolis and we told Governor Rudy Perpich, 'We'd like you to call special session of the legislature,'" said Hutchinson. "This was not a minor event, and he agreed to do it. And then the question was, how do we help the legislators determine that this is the right thing to do? Our goal was to try to rally support both in the legislature and in the larger community."

A poll taken at the time showed 85 percent of the state's residents favored changing the law to make hostile takeovers of Minnesota companies more difficult.[5] Members of the arts community and social action groups supported by the Dayton Hudson foundation flooded Hutchinson with calls asking how they could help. He hastily called a meeting at the Children's Theater in Minneapolis. "The CEO said, 'This is stupidest thing I can ever imagine doing—we're going to get in trouble.' We went ahead anyway. There were no speeches or anything—it was just a Q & A session," Hutchinson said. "People wanted to know what was happening—people didn't know what an arbitrageur was. Fundamentally, none of us understood that this company could disappear.

"The place was completely full. At one point, inevitably, somebody raised his hand and said, 'What should we do?' And I said, 'It's not our job to tell people what they ought to do—it's up to you.' And a woman stands up and says, 'I'll tell you what to do—call the governor's office!' and she reads off the number. So in a conversation with each other, they created what they would do." Soon after, a besieged Terry Montgomery, the governor's chief of staff, phoned Hutchinson. "He said, 'You've got to get these people to stop calling! I don't want to talk to one more ballet company or art museum administrator!' I told him that I couldn't turn it off, because I didn't turn it on."

The state assembly subsequently passed the measure and the governor signed it into law. "One legislator called me up and said, 'How could I vote any other way? My mom called me up and told me after 34 years she took her vacuum cleaner back to Dayton's because it broke—and they took it back!'" Hutchison laughed. "So it was both good customer service and the community relationship." The Hafts never got a chance to test the new law. In October 1987, the stock market crashed. The Dow Jones Industrials lost more than 22 percent in a day, and Dayton Hudson shares nose-dived to $30. Speculators who had borrowed funds to get a piece of the takeover action now faced margin calls, and the market meltdown killed potential financing for the deal. The Hafts withdrew their offer. Various reports estimated their loss on the Dayton Hudson takeover attempt between $60 million and $70 million. Meanwhile, the retailer jumped on the opportunity to repurchase 15 percent of its common shares. By 1989, its earnings had rebounded 80 percent from their 1987 level, to $410 million, and the stock skyrocketed to nearly $74 a share.[6]

"I will tell you the interesting fallout from this," Hutchinson said. "Before the Dart challenge, there was serious discussion about whether or not we ought to maintain the 5 percent [charitable giving] policy. This was 1986 through 1987, and there was a big discussion going on about where we were headed and who we were going to be. After the meeting at the theater and the legislation passed and the Hafts went away—end of discussion. It was, I thought, the best living proof in this country that being a good corporation in every sense—good to your customers, good to your employees, good to your communities—would be good for you. I don't think companies often get the chance to learn that; it's an act of faith in more cases than not. Here was living proof it worked."

ALL IN THE FAMILY

Perhaps the Hafts were thwarted by the spirit of George Draper Dayton, a man who walked by faith in all of his business ventures. As early as 1909, the banker, real estate investor, and department store owner placed his Minneapolis properties in a trust, with an eye to endowing a foundation. On August 27, 1918, Dayton, his wife Emma, his children and their spouses gathered to formally establish the Dayton Foundation. According to the minutes of the first meeting, George Draper Dayton offered a prayer "thanking the heavenly father that the hour had been reached when the Foundation could be established, and asking that future trustees be chosen who will faithfully guard the interest and perform the work of the foundation. . . . The Foundation should live for centuries."[7] Dayton provided an endowment of $1 million; $900,000 from the sale of properties, and $100,000 in cash. Its purpose was "to aid in promoting the welfare of mankind anywhere in the world . . . by affording opportunities for education . . . by bettering the physical habits and conditions of human living, and by relieving the distress and ministering to the needs of the poor, the sick and the afflicted."[8] None of the Dayton family members drew a salary.

In its early years, the foundation supported institutions that permeated Dayton's life—a variety of Presbyterian churches, seminaries and foreign missionaries; the YMCA; Macalester College. Other recipients included the Minneapolis Council of Social Agencies, Goodwill Industries, the Boys and Girls Clubs, Tuskegee Institute, The American Foundation for the Blind and the Minneapolis Art Museum.[9] Some of the donations were personal: A former colleague suffered financial ruin late in life and his family could not afford a marker for his grave. Dayton sent $400 to pay for a white marble headstone.[10]

In 1946, Dayton's son, George Nelson, formalized the long-standing policy of giving away 5 percent of the store's pretax profits—the second company in the nation to do so, and the most giving allowed by federal law at the time (in 1981 the Reagan Administration boosted the limit to 10 percent). "The health of community in which you're operating is as important as the way you operate," said G.N.'s son, Bruce Dayton. "That was the way we were brought up. Our grandfather and father were very civic-minded people. We worked hard to develop Target's [philanthropy], and that's why the Target giving program now keeps

those communities healthy and nurtures their social atmosphere."
Douglas Dayton said his father wasn't a particular fan of the arts
or music, "but he was generous to them. He said if we didn't have
these things, we'd be just another cow town."

In the 1970s, the Dayton brothers hired the late Wayne Thompson, former city manager of Oakland, California, to lead the
foundation. Robert MacGregor, a former Minneapolis city councilman, was Thompson's right-hand man. "The foundation had
been really a family affair," he recalled. "The company was becoming national, and the brothers wanted it to be run more professionally. We used to say that we were in the business of ringing
cash registers, and they would ring more often and louder if our
communities were healthy. We were charged with not just giving
away money, but providing leadership."

One of Thompson's first ideas was a recreational camp for
inner-city kids. The foundation located an abandoned government
facility in the woods of northern Minnesota and funded renovations, adding a swimming pool. Thompson and MacGregor then
rallied a group of public partners: The YMCA signed on to manage the facility, the city provided maintenance, and the school
board agreed to run an educational program. It quickly became the
largest camp in Minnesota, MacGregor said.

Another early effort involved college students. "At the time of
the Vietnam War there were an awful lot of angry people on college campuses," MacGregor recalled. "There was a growing gap
between business leaders and the college campus. John D. Rockefeller III had an idea. He wanted senior business leaders and leaders on university campuses to find a project to do together.
Rockefeller ran into Bruce Dayton—and Bruce gave the project to
Wayne and me. We invited Rockefeller to the University of Minnesota—I can see him today, sitting in a rocking chair talking to
students, and he charmed them. We put together a three-day

retreat at a Lutheran camp in rural Minnesota with leaders from all the major campuses in Minnesota and ten CEOs of major companies in the state."

After a series of discussions, the two sides agreed on a project to develop the Minneapolis riverfront. The city borders the Mississippi, but there was no public access to it at the time. "We had 1,000 young people working on this thing and they did a fantastic job," said MacGregor. Burlington Northern donated railroad ties to build walking paths, Dayton's provided trucks to deliver supplies, and the city got involved as well. It kicked off the redevelopment of the riverfront as a public amenity.

On the leadership side, the Daytons and the foundation made a mission of encouraging more generous giving from other corporations. Kenneth Dayton, in partnership with the Chamber of Commerce, started the Keystone Club—made up of companies who gave away 5 percent of pretax profits, MacGregor said. Dayton gave speeches around the country urging other firms to join. "The tradition of Dayton Hudson was then picked up all over the country by organizing 5 percent clubs and 2 percent clubs," MacGregor said. "Some cities did a better job than in the Twin Cities."

As the years went on, the foundation formalized its grant-giving focus: 40 percent went to social action, 40 percent to the arts, and 20 percent to everything else, including education and the environment, according to Hutchinson, who succeeded Thompson and MacGregor in running the foundation. The Dayton Hudson foundation supported the United Way, the Urban League, the Urban Coalition, and small community-based organizations. "We did a ton of work oriented toward moving families off welfare and into work," and improving the access to, and quality of, daycare, Hutchinson recalled. The arts program supported established symphonies, operas, and museums as well as small developing arts organizations where the company operated stores.

Completely apart from the foundation, the Daytons leveraged the efforts of employees to improve the community. B. Dalton bookstores ran nationwide literacy programs for adults. Target's store managers got involved in local philanthropy and helped direct grants in their communities. The corporation's senior executives served on nonprofit boards. "Everybody was expected to be engaged in the community," said Hutchinson. "One of my jobs was to help senior executives figure out where they could best be engaged."

In the 1990s, after Dayton Hudson sold off its specialty stores, the remaining operating divisions of the company concentrated on areas of giving related to their missions. There were actually four separate giving programs: The corporation itself, the department stores, Target, and Mervyn's. Target focused on families, Mervyn's championed women's issues, and the corporation retained a strong focus on job training and the arts. The giving became more and more decentralized as the company grew, said Chris Park, who ran the charitable organization in the first half of the 1990s. "We tried to pick values the community would resonate with, engaging the local [Target] store managers in decision making; 99.9 percent of time we financed what they thought was important," she said. Target also recruited vendors as partners in various initiatives. In one case, Hershey's donated a percentage of candy sales to a program known as "Helping Hugs," which purchased and distributed teddy bears to police and fire stations to give to children during a crisis (a program widely copied).

CAUSE MARKETING

Meanwhile, marketing guru John Pellegrene forged closer ties with the foundation, Park recalled. "During my time the relationship with advertising really got strong and they bought into using it as a differentiator for company," she said. Singer Amy Grant did a series of commercials discussing the 5 percent policy, putting a public face on corporate giving. Promotions highlighting the policy are prominent in Target stores. Customers have noticed. Laura Noss is founder of Social Planets, a San Francisco communications firm that works with the nonprofit sector. "It makes a big difference," she said. "Even before I became a Tarzhay devotee, I felt a little bit better about getting a great deal, because a portion was going back into community. They really go out into the community. I was driving through East Palo Alto, which is a pretty economically disadvantaged area, and here were kids wearing bright red Target T-shirts and cleaning up the side of road. The only reason I knew it was Target is they had a big bull's-eye on the back of the shirt. Community philanthropy has been increasingly important to me, because through my own business I can see what the larger business community can do when they are committed."

Pellegrene's relationship with the foundation spawned the Take Charge of Education program in 1997, in which charge card holders can donate 1 percent of purchases to the school of their choice. "The Target education [program] works because they've sort of taken themselves out of the middle and said, 'You shop here, you tell us where you want the money to go and we'll get it there,'" Hutchinson said. "Does it have positive public relations value to Target? Sure. But it's concrete, it's real, it's tangible, people can see it. And they like that." In January 2000, when the corporation's name was changed to Target, it consolidated all of the giving into the Target Foundation, although each division maintains its own program under that umbrella.

Target still gives away 5 percent of pretax income, making it one of the most generous corporate programs in the country. The median ratio of U.S. corporate contributions to domestic pretax income was just 1 percent in 1999, according to the most recent data available from the Conference Board's annual report on corporate contributions. *Business Ethics* magazine has named Target one of its "100 Best Corporate Citizens."

ENVIRONMENTAL EFFORTS

Meanwhile, Target's reputation is growing among customers concerned about environmentally sound practices. The U.S. Environmental Protection Agency, the National Recycling Coalition, and the American Plastics Council have called the retailer a leader in waste reduction.[11] In 1994, it launched a program to eliminate extra packaging, particularly in clothing, which also made it more efficient to get goods on the floor. Target says between 1994 and 2001 it reduced the waste generated per dollar of sales by 33 percent. The company also refurbishes and reuses more than 450 million clothes hangers and recycles 20,000 damaged shopping carts a year.[12] Target customer Stephanie Sonnenfeld said she bought a bright red dog food bowl made from a recycled cart for her chow, Buddha. "I like that concept. I'm not the most environmentally conscious person, but I thought that was a good idea." In meetings with designers, Target staffers sip their coffee from oversized, stylish, plastic cups supplied by the company, instead of disposable ones.

For Peter Hutchinson, the former foundation director, Target's long-time legacy as an ethical corporation was confirmed in the painful takeover battle with the Dart Group back in 1987. "One of the early lessons for me in this work was you do community involvement because community involvement is strategically important for the company," Hutchinson said. "If you try to do it for any other reason, you're worse off, because people see it as just shameless public relations. No one is interested in shameless public relations. What they want to see is the real stuff, real engagement, real involvement. I don't think we were successful in beating the takeover because of what we did then. I think we were successful because of what we did in the preceding 40 years."

⊙ CHECK OUT

Philanthropy

Endowment: In 1918, George Draper Dayton endowed a family foundation with a $1 million gift, which focused heavily on organizations affiliated with the Presbyterian church and community groups.

Formal policy: In 1946, George Nelson Dayton formalized the long-standing policy of giving away 5 percent of pretax profits—the most giving allowed by federal law at the time.

1970s: The five Dayton brothers, grandsons of the founder, hired professional managers to run the foundation, focusing primarily on projects in Minnesota; the Daytons encouraged other companies to give away 2 percent or 5 percent of pretax profits.

1980s: The foundation's focus broadened geographically as the company expanded. The foundation devoted 40 percent of giving to social action, particularly welfare-to-work and daycare initiatives; 40 percent to the arts; and 20 percent to a mix of causes, including education and the environment. Employees also volunteered for a range of causes, including literacy. In 1987, the community rallied to help the company defeat a hostile takeover attempt.

1990s: Giving became more strategically aligned with the business focus of each division; for example, Target emphasized the family and Mervyn's concentrated on women's issues. The company began promoting its philanthropy and giving customers a direct say in donations through its Take Charge of Education program. Target also focused on environmental practices such as reducing waste packaging and recycling damaged shopping carts.

CHAPTER 11

Challenges

> Brands need to be elected by
> people every day—it's like a politician.
> If you forget that your survival depends
> on the consumers voting with their
> wallets, you're dead.
>
> —Marc Gobé, co-founder, Desgrippes
> Gobé Group, New York

TAPPED OUT

By the fourth quarter of 2002, it appeared the American consumer—whose spending had kept the U.S. economy from toppling into recession—was finally tapped out. Credit card debt, home foreclosures, and bankruptcies surpassed historic highs during the year. Consumer confidence crumbled and the stock market swooned on disappointing corporate earnings, slow job growth, and the threat of war with Iraq. Mass retailers, which had outperformed their upscale counterparts all year, began to feel the pinch. In November 2002, Target's same-store sales fell 5.7 percent, and in December slipped another .3 percent, well below goals. Apparel and accessories were especially weak; consumers instead spent money on basics like pharmaceuticals and food. Wal-Mart, Federated Stores, and a number of specialty retailers all experienced disappointing results in the crucial holiday season as well. Target's stock ended the year at $30, off 27 percent in 2002. The upscale discounter would clearly face some tough quarters ahead. And those were just the short-term tribulations.

FOOD FIGHT

Longer term, the company is confronting significant challenges, foremost among them, its SuperTarget growth strategy. In 2001, Target had 62 of the discount store/supermarket combos, with plans to operate a total of 300 by the end of the decade. That strategy puts it squarely in the path of its 800-pound Arkansas nemesis, Wal-Mart. In 2002, some 60 percent of SuperTarget locations overlapped with Wal-Mart.[1] But size-wise, it's the equivalent of a one-on-one competition between Shaquille O'Neal and Dr. Ruth

Westheimer. By October 2002, Wal-Mart had more than 1,150 Supercenters—making it the nation's largest grocery chain—and said it would build at least 200 more in 2003.[2] If Wal-Mart Supercenters blast forward on their current trajectory, they will outnumber SuperTargets by roughly nine-to-one at the end of the decade.

That kind of scale brings a scary amount of buying power, which helps make up for the notoriously pitiful margins in the grocery business. For example, outsiders estimate Target makes a profit of 9 percent on nonfood goods, and just 2 percent on groceries, according to *Forbes*.[3] Moreover, Wal-Mart currently owns its grocery warehouses, which add about 16 percent to its costs; Target depends on wholesalers Supervalu and Fleming to distribute goods, adding 21 percent in expenses.[4]

Target says its productivity is on par at its SuperTarget stores. The company is betting it can compete with Wal-Mart in food the same way it does in its traditional stores—with style. The 40,000-sq.-ft. markets offer deluxe bakeries, fresh sushi, Starbucks boutiques—even a Fuji apple screened for sweetness, using an infrared scanner that checks the sugar level.[5] Target also has been boosting the offerings under its private label grocery line, Archer Farms. But will customers notice? "Defining fashion in food is a far more challenging requirement than defining fashion in home furnishings and apparel," said Sanford Bernstein analyst Emme Kozloff.

The groceries are something of a loss leader to get consumers in the door more often, where hopefully, they'll buy more nonfood items. Dallas Target customer Melodie Layman said that's how it works for her: She used to grocery shop and then meander over to the other aisles for apparel, housewares or workout tapes. She realized she was spending so much time there, her ice cream was melting in the check out line. "I started realizing if I got groceries first then I spent too much time afterwards the stuff was going to spoil," she said. "Now I always spend my last hour getting groceries."

Target's internal surveys show that 40 percent of food shoppers at SuperTarget use the store as their main grocery store, according to Deborah Weinswig, retail analyst with Salomon Smith Barney. "I would assume over time, especially as shoppers become more aware of it, you'll see a higher return on capital," she said. "Target is not union, so it can charge lower prices than other food retailers. In the Northeast, SuperTargets have done extremely well."

EXPANSION WOES

But inevitably the question is not, "If they build them, will customers come?" but rather, "Can they build them at all?" The company's fastest growth is in the Northeast and Mid-Atlantic States, where it has encountered serious opposition to its megastores. The largest formats have drawn the ire of antigrowth advocates who don't want big-box retailers in their neighborhoods. "People used to say, 'We want you to build it but not in my backyard,'" CEO Robert Ulrich told *Stores Magazine* in May 2001. "We called them NIMBYs [not in my backyard]. Now we've got BANANAs: ban anything new anywhere near anything. Twenty-two states have passed laws to contain suburban development in the past three years, and the antigrowth lobby won't be happy until they make it impossible for big-box stores to get new building permits."[6] Earlier that year, Ulrich told an industry audience in New York that managed growth was one of the three most important public policy issues facing retailers. "The truth is, goods and services typically follow population growth, not the reverse," Ulrich said. "We won't build a store in a location if the population and other factors aren't there to support it. That seems obvious to us, but apparently not to some planning commissions. In theory, we all agree that people have a right to decide where they want to live. But in practice, when people move to second-tier suburbs, and business goes there to serve them, the alarmists call it urban sprawl."[7]

Stacy Mitchell, a researcher at the Institute for Local Self Reliance and author of *The Hometown Advantage: How to Defend Your Main Street Against Chain Stores and Why it Matters* (ILSR, February 2000), contends that when a big box comes in, businesses *currently* serving the community are undermined. "They are shifting sales away from locally owned businesses, consuming large amounts of land and exacerbating auto use, which increases air pollution," she said. "And there are a growing number of abandoned big-box stores around the country—Wal-Mart has 400— which is a pretty glaring indication of their lack of concern and commitment to the local community." Mitchell also argues that the big boxes have a negative impact on the labor force, offering low-wage, nonunion jobs locally, and putting pressure on U.S. manufacturers to ship jobs overseas. She cites Black & Decker's decision to close a number of plants and move operations to Asia as one example.

CONTROVERSY OVERSEAS

Target's use of overseas labor to make its private-label goods is another controversial challenge for the corporation. In 1999, four labor rights groups filed a federal class-action lawsuit against Target and 26 other prominent retailers, including Gap, J.C. Penney, Nordstrom, and Sears, charging mistreatment of workers in the

Northern Mariana Islands, a U.S. commonwealth in the western Pacific known as Saipan. In September 2002, seven retailers, including Target, settled the suit without admitting wrongdoing (23 others had settled earlier). The deal creates a $20 million fund to pay back wages to workers and create a monitoring system to prevent labor abuses.[8]

Target vice president and general counsel James T. Hale said his company signed the settlement only because litigation would have been too costly. "It is a sad fact that these lawsuits were never about the public good," Hale said in a statement. "They were simply one more instance of class-action lawyers acting as publicity profiteers by using the media to smear a company's reputation without regard for the truth."[9] (The plaintiff's lead attorney, Milberg, Weiss, Bershad, Hynes & Lerach, waived more than $10 million in fees in the case.) One remaining defendant, San Francisco-based Levi Strauss & Co., stopped doing business on the island soon after the suit was filed and is the last holdout in the case. Levi spokeswoman Linda Butler told the *Los Angeles Times*, "The allegations are simply not true, and we believe that settling untrue claims compromises our company's values."[10]

The lawsuit, which claimed Target was the second largest producer in Northern Marianas, accused the companies of using indentured labor—predominantly young women from Asia—who were denied basic human rights. According to the *LA Times*, the seven retailers vowed they would not settle when earlier deals were reached, but they suffered two major legal setbacks in May 2002.[11] A U.S. District Court judge ruled that all garment workers on the island could sue the retailers as a class, even though their work experiences might have varied significantly, the *LA Times* said. Judge Alex R. Munson, based in Saipan, also allowed the earlier settlement to proceed over the objections of the seven companies.[12]

As a U.S. commonwealth, Saipan must abide by all U.S. laws. But in 1989, minimum wage was lowered and immigration rules relaxed to promote economic development. Labor advocates say factory owners have recruited workers from China, Taiwan, and the Philippines, who pay fees of up to $5,000 for the work opportunity, and then spend years paying them back. Many also were charged $100 a month for food and an equal amount for lodging, according to the *LA Times*.[13] The Department of Labor has slapped multimillion-dollar fines against numerous Saipan factory owners for wage and hour violations. "Although some progress has been made, we continue to see substantial violations and obviously need to continue our efforts in Saipan," department spokeswoman Sue Hensley told the *LA Times*.[14]

Nicaragua has been another region beset with labor troubles. Labor rights groups claim Target produces several private-label lines at factories in Nicaragua's Las Mercedes free trade zone. Labor advocates say workers put in 14 hours a day, six days a week, and receive wages of about $80 a month, which is below the poverty level, and that a fund that is set aside for worker health care has been corrupted by the factories.[15]

In January 2000, at the Mil Colores plant in Managua, workers who tried to unionize were fired. To protest the firings, remaining employees organized a work stoppage, leading to beatings and a few arrests, and Mil Colores subsequently fired 200 workers and pressed criminal charges against 68 people who had joined the protest.[16] Pedro Ortega, head of the Federation of Textile, Garment, Leather and Shoe Workers in Nicaragua, visited Minneapolis in 2000, hoping to ask Target officials to lean on suppliers to allow Nicaraguan workers to organize. His visit was funded by the U.S.-based Mid Atlantic Campaign for Labor Rights and supported by the Minnesota Fair Trade Coalition. Target, which refused the meeting, said it had commissioned auditors to check conditions at Mil Colores, and found no evidence "supporting allegations of abusive working conditions," adding that the audit did not address management/labor issues. "We do not believe that is an appropriate Target Corporation role."[17]

Marc Gobé of Desgrippes Gobé Group said globalization is presenting a daunting series of new challenges for U.S. corporations. "You can't be good at home and bad outside of the country," he said. "We've done a lot of study on Generation Y. They are seriously a strong group of activists and very involved in monitoring business practices and political issues. If you want to practice business in the future, on the one side you need to be concerned about your image as good citizen, but also about how you operate outside of the country, and even how the brand is portrayed in countries that don't have the standard of living we have here. The more you participate in what your customers are concerned about, the more you create loyalty."

CREDIT CARDS AND DEPARTMENT STORES

Target has focused on creating loyalty at home through its credit card business—particularly the new Visa Smart Card. But investors tend to look at the operation and judge it against other credit card companies, which typically receive lower valuations than retailers. In 2002, issuers of plastic were experiencing increasing troubles with bad debt, and some of that concern weighed on Target's stock. But Bernstein analyst Emme Kozloff called it an unfair comparison, since Target operates so conservatively. Its bad-debt reserves, for example, are three times the size of traditional credit card companies. Moreover, it has cherry-picked its best Guest Card customers for the Visa program, so the customer quality is higher. Target argues the card is a marketing juggernaut that will connect it more closely with customers and lure them into the store more frequently.

The company's department stores present some of the same challenges: Where investors perceive a liability that should be sold off, Target sees ancillary benefits. Although they make up less than 20 percent of Target Corporation's business, Marshall Field's and Mervyn's sales are indeed on the decline: Revenues fell 4.8 percent at Field's and 1.7 percent at Mervyn's in fiscal 2001. But Mark Miller, analyst with William Blair & Company in Chicago, said the department stores provide paybacks that go beyond the financial performance of the businesses. "They do give the company a human capital and knowledge base that gives [Target stores] their ability to be fashion-forward and trend right," he argued. "The department stores also provide scale for the credit operation—they carry quite a bit of the overhead cost of that business as well. Target [executives] have been good stewards of capital in that they haven't invested a lot in these businesses, and have made every effort to maximize cash flow from these businesses."

In addition, Emme Kozloff said the department stores help demonstrate that Target Corporation understands upscale merchandising, giving it better entrée to brands for the discount division. "It gives them credibility; manufacturers know they won't trash a brand by presenting poorly; they understand how to protect and market a brand," she said. By contrast, she explained, "if [high-end maternity wear designer] Liz Lange did a deal with Wal-Mart, they'd throw the stuff on a rounder with 50 other items." The department stores also generate lots of cash, which the company can use to expand Target stores.

TOO COOL?

There is no question that since 1962, Target has built its business on being the coolest store in the discount landscape. But some question whether there is a liability in basing the business on style differentiation when consumers are such a fickle lot. Moreover, some industry insiders complain that Target's management is arrogant and condescending, which could lead to its downfall.

"Brands need to be elected by people everyday—it's like a politician," said branding expert Marc Gobé. "If you forget that your survival depends on the consumers voting with their wallets, you're dead. And lot of brands think they are so good, they get arrogant and forget to focus on what the customer wants, and what made them great in the first place. That happened to Gap—when you build 1,000 stores and there is one every 500 yards, you become a commodity. When you start changing communications every season because no one is focused on what the brand should be about, and you think you're so hot people will shop your [stores] everywhere—you forget you're not that special and people can copy you."

Kozloff said staying on trend is a delicate balancing act. "By its very nature, anything that gets hot will come down in terms of brand affinity," she explained. "Consumers are finicky. Old Navy and Gap got way too hot and then ice cold. Target has to keep the balance of supporting [the brand] with ad campaigns, without getting too separated from what they sell."

Cynthia Cohen, retail consultant and founder of Strategic Mindshare, argued that Target is less vulnerable than a chain like Gap, because consumers will always be attracted to Target's low-priced household staples, and the chain would have to swerve off course dramatically to alienate those customers. "The one advantage is that Target isn't 100 percent dependent upon fashion," she said. "If Target changed their pricing, they would risk their whole strategy. But everyone buys shampoo, potato chips, and toilet paper. Target right now is cooler than going to the supermarket in many cases. Gap's problem was that they got uncool from a fashion point of view—I went in and there was nothing I wanted. If there is a day I walk into Target when there's nothing I want, and the stores get dirty, disorganized, the merchandise is out of stock, or register lines get too long . . . well, there's no question that anybody can fall off the pedestal."

Salomon Smith Barney's Deborah Weinswig said she's not concerned: "I think maybe they should be arrogant, because they are posting numbers everyone else wishes they were posting." Historically at least, the company's leaders have been aware of the risks of overconfidence: "As we get bigger, can we keep the knowledge of who we are, and the commitment, from the junior levels on up, to do the best job possible? There's a real danger we can get too self-confident and cocky. We may just have to learn how to regain our humility the hard way," fretted Bruce Allbright back in December 1978.[18] If the current leaders guiding Target into the future have similar concerns, they haven't voiced them publicly.

Meanwhile, competition in retail remains as fierce as ever. Wal-Mart is intent on elbowing its way into Target's high-end customer base, and for good reason. Target's fashion items give it the flexibility to charge more, and that means higher gross margins: 31 percent, versus 21 percent for Wal-Mart, according to Kozloff. "Wal-Mart is really trying hard to push the fashion envelope, and they've been doing a much better job," she said. "But their business model does not lend itself to [fashion] merchandise and cultivating brands. Target has put the marketing campaigns out there, so there is a perception that it's a higher-end place. At Wal-Mart the aisles are narrower, the product is piled high and deep, and they're difficult to navigate. Wal-Mart is more of a hunting mission and a lot of people just don't like that."

In the summer of 2003, Kmart is expected to emerge from bankruptcy, some 18 months after filing Chapter 11. The retailer will be smaller and presumably more nimble, with a flashy ad campaign to support its revamped stores (some television spots were directed by filmmaker Spike Lee). "We are not going to try to be Wal-Mart. We're not going to try to be Target," Kmart chairman James B. Adamson told *The Detroit News*. "Kmart is the store of the neighborhood, and we have to capitalize on that."[19] The question is, what will the "store of the neighborhood" offer to entice the neighborhood into the store?

"There's not room enough for everybody in the discount business, but there's room enough for everybody who is really good at *something*," said Allan Pennington, former vice president of corporate development at Dayton Hudson Corporation. "Wal-Mart is really good at allowing people to buy basics cheaply—they're better than anybody at it. Target is good at the fashion aspect of the discount world. The one that there is no room for is Kmart, because Kmart isn't good at anything: It can't compete with Wal-Mart on a cost basis, and it can't compete with Target on a fashion basis, so there's no reason for them to be there." Gobé described Kmart in a line borrowed from "Rain Man," the film starring Dustin Hoffman as an autistic man (with particular preferences in retail): "Kmart sucks."

But that doesn't mean Target can rest easy, he added. "Target is in its early maturing phase," Gobé said. "Within a couple years they will be entering a maturing phase—and at that point they need to think about reinvention so they don't lose their edge. Target's story of survival is to be the hippest version of Wal-Mart—if they lose that, there's no reason for anyone to go there. They need to keep innovating."

If history is any benchmark, Target will continue to innovate. Adversity seems to have brought out the best in the can-do retailer from Minnesota over the years. "There is no strategy we launched or bought that worked, other than Target," founding president Douglas Dayton said. "Target was a completely open-ended job. How far and how fast we could grow was completely under our control. It was up to us what we could do because the field was wide open. Obviously, they have taken it to great heights; it's a more sophisticated, complicated operation now than it used to be. They should be proud of what they've done. Look at all the casualties, people who couldn't figure it out." Target has thrived because it was rooted in the dreams of a great merchant, and blessed with a legacy of high style, ethical values, community service, and professional management. If it continues to keep customers at the center of its vision and remains authentic to its roots, it can count on growth. The only question is how far, and how fast.

⊙ CHECK OUT

Challenges

Getting its SuperTarget model to work: Although groceries drive greater frequency in store traffic, they are also traditionally a lower-margin business than general merchandise—and Wal-Mart is a tough price competitor. Target is trying to apply its fashion sense to food, a complicated proposition.

Expansion: Some 22 states have passed zoning regulations in the last few years restricting the growth of big-box retailers.

Labor issues: A new generation of activists is making the public aware of the impact of U.S. companies overseas. Target will have to closely monitor the companies manufacturing its goods to maintain its reputation among customers as a good corporate citizen.

Credit cards: Target's fast-growing credit card division could hurt its stock valuation; although the retailer has long experience conservatively managing revolving debt, it's a business investors don't understand particularly well.

Department stores: Performance has been declining in recent years, dragging on overall profitability; if Target eventually wants to sell the divisions, it needs to rev up the volume and the valuation of Marshall Field's and Mervyn's.

Balancing its image with the store experience: Target ads are cutting-edge; the company needs to make sure they don't get so edgy that customers follow the hype into the store and feel disappointed by the actual retail experience.

Staying hot without getting burned: Consumers are notoriously fickle; trends that go up generally come down. If Target gets too hot, it risks a meltdown.

Target Corporation Financial Facts

Fiscal year ending 2/2/02, numbers are rounded; Source: annual report.

Headquarters: Minneapolis, Minnesota

Founded: 1962 by Dayton's Department Store

Total store count: 1,381
   Target: 1,053
   Marshall Field's: 64
   Mervyn's: 264

One-year change: 5.6%

Retail square footage: 161.3 million
One-year change: 12%

Locations: 47 U.S. states

Employees: 280,000

Sales: $39.9 billion
One-year change: 8%

Net earnings (excluding unusual items): $1.37 billion

One-year change: 8%

Earnings per share (diluted, excluding extraordinary items): $1.51

One-year change: 9.4%

Capital investment: $3.2 billion

(in new store construction, remodeling, technology and distribution)

Executive Officers

Chairman and CEO: Robert Ulrich

Vice Chairman: Gerald Storch

Executive Vice President and CFO: Douglas Scovanner

President, Target Stores: Gregg Steinhafel

President, Marshall Field's: Linda Ahlers

President, Mervyn's: Diane Neal

Target Corporation
Historic Highlights

1857   George Draper Dayton is born in western New York.

1902   Dayton opens Goodfellow's in Minneapolis.

1903   Dayton changes the store's name to the Dayton Dry Goods Company.

1906   Draper Dayton, Dayton's oldest son, named general manager.

1910   Dayton Dry Goods changes its name to The Dayton Company.

1911   George Nelson, Dayton's other son, joins the business.

1918   Dayton Foundation established.

1923   Draper Dayton dies.

1937   George Draper Dayton dies.

1946   Dayton's formalizes corporate giving at 5 percent of pretax profits.

1950   George Nelson Dayton dies; his sons, Donald, Kenneth, Wallace, Bruce, and Douglas take over the business.

1956   Dayton's opens the world's first fully enclosed, two-level shopping center.

1962   Dayton's opens the first Target in Roseville, MN; S.S. Kresge opens the first Kmart in Garden City, MI; Sam Walton opens the first Wal-Mart in Rogers, AR.

1966   Dayton's launches B. Dalton Bookstores.

1967   Dayton's goes public.

1969   Dayton's acquires J.L. Hudson's of Detroit for $150 million in stock; over the next several years it acquires about a dozen specialty retailers which it eventually sells.

1971   Dayton's changes its name to Dayton Hudson Corporation.

1978   Dayton Hudson acquires Mervyn's for $300 million in stock.

1979   Target operates 80 units; sales surpass $1 billion.

1983   Kenneth Dayton retires from executive management, the last Dayton to do so.

1984   Dayton's and Hudson's, which had operated separately, combined to form Dayton Hudson Department Store Company.

1986   Dayton Hudson sells B. Dalton Bookstores to Barnes & Noble for $85 million.

1987   The Dart Group makes a run on Dayton Hudson Corporation, which gets the Minnesota legislature to pass a tough antitakeover law.

1990   Dayton Hudson acquires Marshall Field's; Target opens its first Greatland superstore; launches "fast, fun and friendly" service initiatives.

1992   Target division has 500 stores and more than $10 billion in sales.

1994   Robert Ulrich, Target's chairman and CEO, assumes that title at Dayton Hudson.

1995   Target opens its first SuperTarget store; launches the Guest Card.

1999   Dayton Hudson launches e-commerce division.

2000   Dayton Hudson changes its name to Target Corporation.

2001   Target rolls out Visa Smart Card; operates 1,053 Target stores with nearly $40 billion in revenues.

Notes

Chapter 2: The Right Stuff

1. "Dayton Launches Target," *Discount Store News*, January 1, 1962, p. 2.
2. "Jeans Put Target in Hot Seat," *Discount Store News*, October 8, 1979; reprinted in April 20, 1992, p. 62.
3. Jill Lettich, "A Bloomingdale's Approach to the Discount Market," *Discount Store News*, September 17, 1990, p. 47.
4. Alice Z. Cuneo, "Marketer of the Year: On Target," *Advertising Age*, December 11, 2000, p. 1.
5. Lettich, p. 47.
6. Kathleen M. Eisenhardt and D. Charles Galunic, "Coevolving At Last, a Way to Make Synergies Work," *Harvard Business Review*, January 2000, p. 91.
7. Debbie Howell, "Building a Brand the Target Way: Exclusive and chic far outpace cheap," *DSNRetailing Today*, April 8, 2002, p. 58.

8. Becky Ebenkamp, "John Pellegrene: Top class in Mass," *Brandweek*, October 12, 1998, p. 68.

9. Ibid.

10. "Target Yanks 'Neo-Nazi' Clothing Off Shelves," *Reuters*, August 29, 2002.

11. Richard C. Halverson, "Target Builds a Winning Image" *Discount Store News*, September 17, 1990, p. 44.

12. Teri Agins, "Designers Woo Discounters to Sell Leather Jackets Amid Paper Towels," *Wall Street Journal*, April 24, 2002, p. B1.

13. James Thurman, "Restoration of Washington Icon Is an Attraction in Itself," *Christian Science Monitor*, December 1, 1998, p. 3.

14. Vanessa L. Facenda, "Michael v. Martha: More Than Michael," *Retail Merchandiser*, August 2001, p. 30.

15. John Leland, "A Prefab Utopia: What happens when a furniture company builds a community," *New York Times Magazine*, December 1, 2002.

16. Mark Miller and Dan Hofkin, "Target Corporation," *William Blair & Company basic report*, June 5, 2001, p. 12.

17. "Mossimo, Inc." *Hoovers Online*, June 29, 2002, hoovers.com/premium/profile/7/0,2147,47767,00.html.

18. "Todd Oldham Deal: Minneapolis," *PR Newswire*, September 6, 2001.

19. "Target Stores Announces New Licensing Deal with Ecko Unlimited," *company press release*, December 18, 2001.

20. "Patriotism Unplugged: Target Stores Partner with Fashion Designer Stephen Sprouse for Fourth of July 2002," *company press release*, February 8, 2002.

21. "Groundbreaking New Collection of Consumer Products, Imbuing Everyday Objects with Style, Elegance and Magic, Hails

Starck's 'Democratization of Design,' " *PRNewswire*, April 3, 2002.

22. Agins, p. B1.
23. Mike Duff, "Sizing Up Apparel: Fashion Focus Fits Target to a 'T'," *DSNRetailing* Today, April 8, 2002, p. 61.

Chapter 4: Advertising and Promotion

1. Malcolm Gladwell, *The Tipping Point: How Little Things Can Make a Big Difference,* New York: Little Brown & Company, (February 2000), p. 34, 132, 139.
2. Alice Z. Cuneo, "Marketer of the Year: On Target," *Advertising Age*, December 11, 2000, p. 1.
3. Patricia Winters Lauro, "Peace, Love and Madison Avenue: TV marketers are embracing the sweeter side of the 60's," *New York Times*, December 2, 1999, p. C6.
4. Cuneo, p. 1.
5. Becky Ebenkamp, "John Pellegrene: Top Class in Mass," *Brandweek*, October 12, 1998, p. 68.
6. Dan Mangan and Daniel Schiff, "High-tech PATH Ads Are Tunnel Vision," *New York Post*, June 18, 2002, p. 3.
7. Shelly Branch, "How Target Got Hot: Hip goods and hipper ads are luring the MTV and BMW crowds into the big box," *Fortune*, May 1999, p. 169.
8. Cuneo, p. 1.
9. Ibid.
10. "Take Charge of Education" newsletter, September/October 2002, Target.com website, http://target.com/common/page .jhtml?content=target_cg_tcoe_newsletter.
11. Ebenkamp, p. 1.
12. "Celebrities Boost Target," *Discount Store News*, April 20, 1970 reprinted in April 20, 1992, p. 54.

13. "Newspaper Ads Get a New Look," *Discount Store News*, April 20, 1992, p. 66.

14. Mike Troy, "Debunking the Upscale Myth: Below the surface lies a discount core," *DSNRetailing Today*, April 8, 2002, p. 57.

15. Cuneo, p. 1.

16. Susan Feyder, "New Dayton Hudson CEO Seen as Aggressive, Creative," *Minneapolis Star Tribune*, April 15, 1994, p. 1D.

17. Target.com, http://startsomething.target.com/info/index.asp.

Chapter 5: Service and Technology

1. Laura Liebeck, "Mixing Discipline with Disney," *Discount Store News*, Sept. 17, 1990, p. 66A.

2. Ibid.

3. Ibid.

4. Leonard A. Schlesinger and James L. Heskett, "The Service Driven Service Company," *Harvard Business Review*, September/October 1991, p. 10.

5. Mark Schoifet and Heidi Gralla, "Right on Target: The Marshall Field's acquisition bolstered Dayton Hudson's department store business, but the big plans are for its discount chains," *Shopping Centers Today*, November 1990, p. 27.

6. Constance L. Hays, "Can Target Thrive in Wal-Mart's Cross Hairs?" *New York Times*, June 9, 2002, p. D1.

7. Ibid.

8. "EDI: Internet Revolutionizes EDI," *Discount Store News*, May 24, 1999, p. 5.

9. "Target Exec Blasts Redundant Exchange Efforts," *Chain Store Age Executive*, August 2001, p. 80.

10. Gregg Andrews, "Target's New CRM System Should Enhance Cross-Selling Opportunities," *National Jeweler*, June 1, 2001, p. 38.

11. Bob Tedeschi, "Discount Giants Learn Online Lessons: Film, Yes; Shampoo, No," *New York Times*, September 26, 2001, p. E6.

12. Chana R. Schoenberger, "Bull's-Eye: Target has solved the mystery of how to make the Web work for a mass retailer," *Forbes*, Sept. 2, 2002, p. 76.

13. Greg Johnson, "Fighting for Dollars on the Net: Traditional merchants are proving to be heavy competition for web-only firms," *Los Angeles Times*, November 23, 2001, p. C1.

14. "Target to Deliver Four Unique Brands in One Comprehensive Site at Target.com; Amazon.com to Provide Technology and Fulfillment for Web Site," *PR Newswire*, August 12, 2002.

15. Johnson, p. C1.

16. Stephanie Gaskell, Leah Haines, and Eric Lenkowitz, "Why Did the $4b Man Get a Target Card? To Save an Extra $2.99," *New York Post*, November 30, 2002, p. 9.

17. Deborah Weinswig and Garrett Bruttomesso, "Target Corporation: Giving credit where credit is due," *Bear Stearns Equity Research*, February 22, 2002, p. 11.

18. Ibid.

19. Weinswig and Bruttomesso, p. 7.

20. Hays, p. D1.

21. Mayor Bloomberg donated his percentage to P.S. 40 in Queens, at the suggestion of a shopper behind him in the check out line.

22. Weinswig and Bruttomesso, p. 21.

Chapter 6: The Legend of George Draper Dayton

1. Bruce Dayton and Ellen B. Green, *George Draper Dayton: A Man of Parts,* privately published biography, 1997, p. 241.
2. Shelly Branch, "How Target Got Hot: Hip goods and hipper ads are luring the MTV and BMW crowds into the big box," *Fortune,* May 1999, p. 169.
3. Janet Moore, "Wall Street's Darling: The Ulrich Effect; As retail company basks in a Target-led recovery, CEO Bob Ulrich still must fix the troubled Mervyn's division," *Minneapolis Star Tribune,* March 15, 1998, p. 1A.
4. Sally Apgar, "Dayton Hudson at Crossroads; CEO Ulrich still struggling to jump-start Mervyn's stores," *Minneapolis Star Tribune,* July 23, 1995, p. 1A.
5. Sally Apgar, "Dayton's Due for Makeover: The Man from Target to usher in a new era, but how is the question," *Minneapolis Star Tribune,* June 21, 1994, p. 1A.
6. Dayton and Green, p. 2.
7. Ibid, pp. 2–3.
8. Ibid, p. 11.
9. Ibid, pp. 27–28.
10. Ibid, p. 32.
11. Ibid, pp. 39–40.
12. Ibid, p. 36.
13. Ibid, p. 56.
14. Ibid, p. 60.
15. Ibid, p. 355.
16. Ibid, p. 195.
17. Ibid, pp. 104–105.
18. Ibid, p. 106.
19. Ibid, p. 115.

20. Ibid, p. 212.

21. Ibid, p. 242.

22. "The Daylight Store: Opening of splendid new store of good-fellow Dry Goods Co., corner Seventh and Nicollet," *Minneapolis Journal*, June 25, 1902, p. 7.

23. Dayton and Green, p. 246.

24. Ibid, p. 261.

25. Ibid, p. 256.

26. Ibid, p. 263.

27. Ibid, p. 267.

28. Ibid, p. 271.

29. Ibid, pp. 366–367.

30. Ibid, p. 302.

31. Ibid, p. 308.

32. Ibid, p. 323.

Chapter 7: The Next Generation

1. Wayne Christensen, "The Decade of the Daytons: The downtown dynasty has influence far beyond the department store walls," *Corporate Report*, January 1979, p. 38.

2. Witold Rybczynski, "The New Downtowns," *The Atlantic Monthly*, May 1993, pp. 99–100

3. Paul Doocey, "Twelve Who Dared to Be Bolder, Brighter, Better," *Shopping Centers Today*, May 1991, p. 47.

4. Rybczynski, p. 100.

5. "Northland's Client: Hudson's department store and the five Webbers who run it," *Architectural Forum*, June 1954, p. 129.

6. Walter Guzzardi Jr., "An Architect of Environments," *Fortune*, January 1962, p. 80.

7. "Victor Gruen: Father of shopping malls, pioneer of urban centers," *Shopping Center World*, May/June 1980, p. 166.

8. Phil Patton, "Agents of Change," *American Heritage*, December 1994, p. 100.

9. "Northland's Sculpture: Fun, fanciful and a little challenging," *Architectural Forum*, June 1954, p. 130.

10. Don Wharton, "Those Amazing Shopping Centers," *Readers Digest*, May 1962, p. 194.

11. "Northland's Client: Hudson's department store and the five Webbers who run it," *Architectural Forum*, June 1954, p. 129.

12. Doocey, p. 47.

13. Ibid.

14. Ibid.

15. "Victor Gruen: Father of shopping malls, pioneer of urban centers," *Shopping Center World*, May/June 1980, p. 166.

16. "Target Born as a Trendsetter," *Discount Store News*, April 20, 1992, p. 37

17. "Target for AMC Meeting," copy of speech provided by Douglas Dayton.

18. "Solemates: The Century in Shoes," From www.century inshoes.com, http://www.centuryinshoes.com/decades/1950/1950.html.

19. Robert Sobel, "Why Pay More?" *Audacity*, Spring 1994, p. 24.

20. Debra J. Pearlstein, *Antitrust Law Developments*, Volume 1, 5th ed., (Chicago: American Bar Association), April 2002, p. 131, footnote 739.

21. Sobel, p. 25.

22. Ibid.

Chapter 8: Management Excellence

1. Duke Ratliff and Jay Johnson, "The Time Machine," *Discount Merchandiser*, September 1997, p. 23.

2. Jean Maddern Pitrone, *Hudson's: Hub of America's Heartland*, (West Bloomfield, MI: Altwerger and Mandel Publishing Company), 1991, p. 134.

3. "Dayton Launches Target," *Discount Store News*, January 1, 1962, p. 2.

4. Ratliff and Johnson, p. 24.

5. "On Target," *company newsletter*, June 1968, Vol. 2, No. 6, p. 1; copy provided by Douglas Dayton.

6. Wayne Christensen, "The Decade of the Daytons: The downtown dynasty has influence far beyond the department store walls," *Corporate Report*, January 1979, p. 41.

7. Ibid, p. 40.

8. "100 Million Seminar," 1968, copy of speech provided by Douglas Dayton.

9. "Facts on the Dayton Corporation," March 4, 1968, document from the *Minneapolis Star Tribune* library.

10. "Merger Bolsters Target," *Discount Store News*, March 24, 1969; reprinted in April 20, 1992, p. 53.

11. Marianne Taylor, "Wal-Mart Acquiring Club Rival," *Chicago Tribune*, November 7, 1990, p. D1.

12. Christensen, p. 132.

13. Jean Maddern Pitrone, *Hudson's: Hub of America's Heartland*, (West Bloomfield, MI: Altwerger and Mandel Publishing Company), 1991, p. 7.

14. Ibid, pp. 10–11.

15. Ibid, p. 25.

16. Vivian M. Baulch, "How J.L. Hudson Changed the Way We Shop," *The Detroit News*, May 19, 1996; http://detnews.com/history/hudson/hudson/htm.

17. Pitrone, p. 40.

18. Baulch, http://detnews.com/history/hudson/hudson/htm.

19. Pitrone, p. 52.

20. Ibid, p. 53.

21. Ibid, p. 56.

22. Baulch, http://detnews.com/history/hudson/hudson/htm.

23. "Hudson's Name Will Fade," *The Associated Press*, January 13, 2001.

24. Witold Rybczynski, "The New Downtowns," *The Atlantic Monthly*, May 1993, p. 100.

25. Pitrone, p. 145.

26. Ibid, p. 150.

27. "Merger Bolsters Target," *Discount Store News*, March 24, 1969; reprinted in April 20, 1992, p. 53.

28. Jennifer Dixon, "Landmark Book Cadillac May Be Razed," *Detroit Free Press*, October 17, 2001, http://www.freep.com/news/locway/booka17_20011017.htm.

29. James E. Sailer and Jay W. Lorsch, "CEO Evaluation at Dayton Hudson," *Harvard Business School Case Study*, 9-491-116, October 15, 1991, p. 8.

30. Christensen, p. 150.

31. "Managers Draft Long Range Plan," *Discount Store News*, June 2, 1969; reprinted in April 20, 1992, p. 54.

32. Ibid.

33. Dick Youngblood, "Dayton Hudson Full Speed Ahead" *Minneapolis Star Tribune*, April 11, 1976, p. 13C.

Chapter 9: Guides for Growth

1. "The First Step: Do it right," *Chain Store Age*, December 1978, p. 76.

2. Laura Liebeck, "Hard Lines Vie for Shelf Space," *Discount Store News*, September 17, 1990, p. 53.

3. Dick Youngblood, "Target Becomes Sales Leader of Dayton Hudson," *Minneapolis Star Tribune*, April 28, 1976, p. 1B.

Chapter 10: Philanthropy

1. Neal St. Anthony and Josephine Marcotty, "Dayton's Seeks Anti-Takeover Aid: Perpich considers calling special session to amend law," *Minneapolis Star Tribune*, June 19, 1987, p. 1A.
2. Ibid.
3. Dick Youngblood, "In Business for the Long Run," *Minneapolis Star Tribune*, June 25, 1990, p. 1D.
4. Ibid.
5. "Statewide Poll Shows 85% Favor Special Session to Protect Dayton Hudson from Hostile Takeover," *Minneapolis Star Tribune* library file, June 23, 1987.
6. Youngblood, p. 1D.
7. "Minutes of the Dayton Foundation," *The Minnesota Historical Society*, The George D. Draper Dayton research files, Collection P2374, August 27, 1918.
8. Bruce Dayton and Ellen B. Green, *George Draper Dayton: A Man of Parts*, privately published biography, 1997, p. 430.
9. Ibid, p. 431.
10. Ibid, p. 438.
11. Jim Konkoly, "Retailer Targets Waste Reduction, Recycling," *Waste News*, Oct 15, 2001, p. 27.
12. Ibid.

Chapter 11: Challenges

1. Debbie Howell, "The Super in SuperTarget: Future format feeds off unique offerings," *DSNRetailing Today*, April 8, 2002, p. 65.

2. Emily Kaiser, "Wal-Mart Sees Record Expansion in 2003," *Reuters Business Report*, October 1, 2002.

3. Kemp Powers, "Kitchen-Sink Retailing: Combine a discount store with a grocery store and what do you get? A disappointing profit margin," *Forbes*, September 2, 2002, p. 78.

4. Ibid.

5. Constance L. Hays, "Can Target Thrive in Wal-Mart's Cross Hairs?" *New York Times*, June 9, 2002, p. D1.

6. Susan Reda, "Boxed In: Growth curbs hit big retailers. Retail companies like Target and Home Depot now find themselves handcuffed by anti-growth lobbyists and encumbered by land-use regulations," *Stores Magazine*, May 2001, p. 42.

7. Ibid.

8. Nancy Cleeland, "Firms Settle Saipan Factory Workers Suit Labor: Activists say the deal will change global corporate treatment of Third World employees," *Los Angeles Times*, September 27, 2002, p. C1.

9. "Target Dismissed from Garment Factory Lawsuits; Company Asserts Class Action Abuse," *company press release*, September 26, 2002.

10. Cleeland, p. C1.

11. Ibid.

12. Ibid.

13. Ibid.

14. Ibid.

15. Doug Grow, "Target Ignoring Unfair-Labor Issues; Retailer Ignores Request to Meet with Nicaraguan Union Activists," *Minneapolis Star Tribune*, June 21, 2000, p. 2B.

16. Ibid.

17. Ibid.

18. "Target: Can it be untracked?" *Chain Store Age*, December 1978, p. 97.

19. Jim Higgins, "Kmart Execs Upbeat: Adamson and Day expect giant retailer to emerge from bankruptcy next summer," *The Detroit News*, September 26, 2002. p. 1B, also online at http://www.detnews.com/2002/business/0209/26/index.htm.

Index